MARATHONS
OF THE WORLD

Updated Edition

Hugh Jones and
Alexander James

IMM **lifestyle**
books™
Read. Learn. Do What You Love.

Contents | From East to West

Introduction

Selecting a limited number of races to be included in this book was a harder task than it might seem. There are now so many marathons in almost every country and territory of the world – from the North Pole and Antarctica to the Sahara Desert, as well as on islands so small that the organisers struggle to set out a 42.2km (26 miles 385 yards) route. The sheer variety on offer dazzles the imagination.

It is hard to believe that the first marathon race (aside from that of the ancient legend) was held little more than a century ago; and the sort of popular running event that we take for granted today only started to emerge in the late 1970s. The Greek legend recounts the story of Pheidippides, a messenger who was sent from the battlefield of Marathon to Athens to deliver news of victory over the Persian army. Exhausted, he expired on arrival, having run a distance now thought to be farther than the modern marathon. The story's romantic appeal inspired Michel Breal, a renowned philologist, to prevail upon his friend Baron Pierre de Coubertin, the founder of the Modern Olympic Games, to include a long-distance race from Marathon to Athens in the inaugural Olympic Games in Greece in the summer of 1896.

Above: Bridges feature in many marathons and offer a spectacular sight from above.

Left: The Rome Marathon is a world-class event with competitors from around the world running through the city.

The first marathon was actually a trial race held a few months before in April 1896 and over the same course. The defining Olympic race played out dramatically and promoters immediately sought to emulate it, primarily in Europe and North America.

The Boston Marathon was born the following year. It has proven the most resilient, maintaining continuity through both world wars and the Great Depression and, after a few shaky years in the 1980s, reinventing itself to follow a more popular formula. In England The Polytechnic Marathon (the 'Poly') from Windsor to Chiswick started in 1909 following the 1908 London Olympic Marathon and was held over a similar course. Many world records were set on this course in the 1950s and 1960s, but the race petered out in the 1990s as the new generation of big city marathons took over.

The 'popular formula' of marathon running was conceived by Fred Lebow, a New Yorker and avid runner, in a fortuitous confluence of circumstances – the running world's 'Eureka' moment. Prior to this date marathons were typically run by a band of elite, usually male, runners who had to complete the course in fast times or were asked to withdraw from the race. Lebow, who had established the New York Marathon in 1970 as a four-lap race within the confines of Central Park, followed up on a suggestion from local distance-runner Ted Corbett to make the race 'citywide'

Above: Clean air and spectacular scenery are just two of the attractions for the Jungfrau Marathon in Switzerland.

in its appeal. City Hall seized upon the idea but misinterpreted it as a proposal to run the race through all five boroughs of the city to celebrate the American bicentennial in 1976. Consequently the field had grown 534 starters in 1975 to total 2,090 participants in just one year. The spectacle it presented enthused enough people to fuel rapid growth, and in 1980 14,000 runners entered the race.

Several of the races included in this book were a direct outgrowth of the New York experience. Even those already in existence, like Berlin, cashed in on the move to city-wide marathon courses. Others, like Stockholm, Barcelona, and London, were set up by those who had been impressed by New York and realized it was an event waiting to happen in other cities of the world.

The 'running boom' as it became known, which started with New York in the late 1970s, caught on in Europe in the early 1980s.

In Japan, marathons were already firmly embedded in the public's awareness: the elite Japanese Fukuoka Marathon had taken over from England's 'Poly' as the place to set world records in the late 1960s. For most Japanese, however, it remained a spectator sport as the field remained closed to all but elite runners. Many Japanese runners travelled abroad to find big-city marathons in which they could take part. Pressure built upon Japanese race organisers to open up their events to mass participation. Finally, after long hard scrutiny of races elsewhere and careful planning, they did just this in 2007 and met with instant success.

By contrast, marathon running was almost unknown in India when the Mumbai Marathon was launched in 2003. By that date marathons had already become far more than just running events and featured carnival aspects including outlandish costumes and huge charity fundraising. Mumbai capitalised on this with supporting events that attracted corporate advertising, cricketing heroes and Bollywood stars. Running, and the Mumbai Marathon with it, became an aspirational pursuit for tens of thousands of people.

Marathons have conquered the world's big cities and are increasingly reaching far more remote locations, specifically aimed at attracting tourist runners. While many of the big-city marathons entice significant numbers of foreigners and contribute heavily to the local economy as a result, others, like the Great Wall Marathon in China, attract an almost exclusively tourist clientele. The Australian Outback Marathon, near Uluru, does the same, even though the overwhelming majority of runners are Australians. The attraction is obvious – if you are adventurous enough to run a marathon, the idea of doing it in an appealing location gives an extra incentive.

I came to marathon running when it was an elite performance sport. People taking up running since the 1980s have done so mainly to participate rather than compete. The two are hardly exclusive of each other, but bring different perspectives. As a non-amateur marathon runner, I ran where I could perform best and where the performance would count for most. That was why I ran in New York, Tokyo, London, Chicago and Beijing, not in the race that offered the most challenging or beautiful course or the most exotic location, but on a fast course in which I could excel. All world records have been set in big-budget races – since these are the events that attract the professional runners. New York was the first such event, paying out large prize money.

Most runners with an eye on the clock will target a 'fast' course at some point in order to obtain the much discussed 'personal best' time, but they may also be attracted to races that hold out the promise of a memorably different experience. For me, the one that offered a completely different experience was the Sahara Marathon. In common with some of the other adventure races in this book, like the Great Wall Marathon or the North Pole Marathon, runners meet up even before arriving at the race. Typically a rapport develops that is only strengthened as the race approaches, with participants sharing accommodation within the homes of the Sahrawi refugees and experiencing the place in a profound way.

Wherever you run, running a marathon allows a deeper sense of participation within a city or country than is open to a visitor with a more casual itinerary, whether at home or abroad. For the social runner, the challenge of running such a long distance will always hold special memories whatever the location. The chance to participate in a race at the same time as the world's elite is appealing: the marathon is the only event where the masses can be on the same course, at the same time, as the best in the world.

Marathons bring a sense of purpose too as you set out on a journey and see it through to the finish. My victory in the second London

Above: The Siberia International Marathon takes place in Omsk, a city closed to foreigners before 1990.

Right: Millennium Park, a landmark of the Chicago Marathon.

Marathon, back in 1982, brought an overwhelming sense of relief. I thought I could do it, other people also seemed to think so, but it was only crossing the finish line that made it reality. Most marathon experiences will be less stark than that and perhaps may be better appreciated and more enjoyable if the runner's concentration is focused on the taking part rather than the end result. For many first-time runners, marathon day may be the end of the journey, preceded by months of mental and physical preparation, training schedules and self-discipline so that the day might be better enjoyed and injury-free. For seasoned runners, who know what their bodies are capable of, achieving a faster marathon time might be the catalyst for entering a race. Whether your finish time is 2½ or 6 hours, the sense of achievement at completing a personal challenge or knocking minutes or seconds off your time can be immense.

The races described in this book offer a huge variety of different experiences. The world is out there waiting for you, and as a marathon runner you are well placed to conquer it. Marathon running involves commitment and a sense of purpose and will be rewarding in whatever circumstances it is realised. Look through these pages for a glimpse of the magical places to which it can transport you.

Hugh Jones

Above: The runners in the Sahara Marathon stay as guests in the refugee camps focusing attention on the plight of the Sahrawi and promoting better understanding.

Auckland Marathon | New Zealand

For most foreign runners the Auckland Marathon is a very long way away, but the event offers something for everyone – with a family run, a 5km race, a quarter, half and full marathons all being staged at the same time. Only the marathon and half marathon cross the Auckland Harbour Bridge, which is the big feature of the course.

The marathon was founded by the YMCA Marathon Club in 1994 as two laps along the Tamaki Drive Waterfront to the east of the city centre. Only when the course was changed to include the Harbour Bridge and the city centre did it generate the international profile the organisers sought. Numbers grew, and now stand at 14,000 with just over half of them women. Of those, 3,000 entries are for the marathon, making it a fairly low-key event when compared to some of the larger marathons. There is an intimate feel to the race that is only partly to do with the limited numbers.

In the pre-dawn, runners board a flotilla of chartered ferries to take them from the city centre across Waitemata Harbour to the start line in Devonport on the north shore. The early start is a sensible solution to the logistical problem of how to get runners from one side of the bridge to the other in the limited time available; the bridge has to be re-opened to general traffic at 9.45am, come what may. Marathon runners set off at 6.10am and the half marathoners follow at 7.00am, giving them a generous cut-off time to reach the crucial 13km (8 mile) point at which they ascend onto the bridge – if they are not there in time they are turned away.

From the start at Torpedo Bay, runners go north on the peninsula turning on to the mainland proper at Takapuna, 8km (5 miles) into the race. They then head south toward the bridge. Descending through Point Erin Park, runners go eastbound along the waterfront to approach the city centre. Before getting there, half marathon runners turn into Victoria Park to finish, but marathon runners bypass the centre by hugging the wharf to emerge on a causeway heading out to a turning point at 30km (18½ miles).

WHILE YOU'RE THERE

Mount Eden is a dormant volcanic crater outside Auckland – once surmounted, it rewards the climber with fabulous views of the city skyline.
For a similar experience, the **Sky Tower**, the country's tallest manmade structure overlooks downtown.
Queen Street and downtown are the best spots for fine dining.
Be sure to check out the city beaches like **Takapuna**.
For an enchanting wildlife experience, take a **dolphin and whale watching tour**. See: www.tourismnewzealand.com

Runners press on to the causeway which the quarter marathon runners, who began outside Victoria Park and turned here for their return to the finish, have cleared by the time the marathon runners arrive. The wealthy waterfront suburbs start from here, and marathon runners can enjoy the spectacular harbour views as they press on for another 5km (3 miles) to the turning point at St Helier Bay.

Retracing the third quarter of the route in reverse to the Victoria Park finish, the 'Party in the Park' welcomes weary finishers with bands, entertainment and a plethora of hospitality tents provided for the estimated 38,000 people attending the celebrations. It is an experience far removed from the peaceful early morning ferry ride across the harbour, but a suitably ebullient end to a hard race. The average time for the course is an impressive 4½ hours, with most runners home while the day is still young.

Right: The Sky Tower looms in the background, an iconic landmark visible throughout the race.

Below: The bridge marks the end of the hilly section of the race, though the incline onto it is the steepest of all.

RACE DETAILS

WHEN? October
WHEN TO APPLY: July
HOW MANY TAKE PART? 15,000
DIFFICULTY RATING: 6/10
SPECIAL CONSIDERATIONS: Hilly at the start but largely flat afterwards. The course can be windy, so keep hydrated.

CONTACT: Auckland Marathon
P.O. Box 37047
Parnell
Auckland, New Zealand
☎ (09) 303 0379
✉ registration@aucklandmarathon.co.nz
🖥 www.aucklandmarathon.co.nz

Sydney Marathon | Australia

The Olympic Games hosted by Sydney in 2000 allowed Australia to project its sport-friendly environment to a watching world. One Olympic legacy that resulted is the Blackmore's Festival of Running Sydney Marathon.

The Sydney Marathon – for short – is the only event arising from the 2000 Olympics that is open to the public. From the first staging it attracted 7,500 runners. The numbers have been growing ever since and it is now one of the most popular sporting events in Australia. The appeal is obvious – you get to run across the iconic Sydney Harbour Bridge and gaze down on the Harbour, the Opera House and the Botanical Gardens as you go.

The finish is at the World Heritage Site of Sydney Opera House, and the great thing about this inclusive running festival is that you get all these impressive sights no matter which running option you choose out of the marathon: the half marathon, the 9km (5½ mile) bridge run and the 4km (2½ miles) family fun run are all staged at the same event. The organisers go to great and varied lengths to live up to their slogan 'The run that's fun for everyone'. The family fun-run route follows a direct track to the Opera House, the bridge run makes a lap out of it, and the marathon and half marathon routes twist around the city centre in intricate webs that feature many hairpin turns. The marathon makes up the required distance by leading runners on a continuously sinuous route to the southeast of the city centre, in and around Centennial Park. The course is undulating but includes several long, flat sections. The weather is generally 19–21°C (66–70°F), with the occasional welcome breeze to help you cool off.

The concept of a running festival, rather than a race, hinges on the idea of making it easy and fun for everyone to take part in one or other of the events on offer. The organisers have clearly achieved this goal, as a total of 30,000 people hit the streets of Sydney, even if some of them do end up walking the entire course.

WHILE YOU'RE THERE

You'll never tire of looking at the beauty of **Sydney Harbour** and its skyline, comprising of the Opera House and bridge – a great way to see it is from the water by taking one of the many ferries that leave the harbour. Keep on the watery track by feasting on the fish market offerings in **Pyrmont**. Or take your fresh food to **Bondi or Coogee Beach** and spark up a barbecue.

Right: The iconic sights of the city are visible in the Sydney Marathon.

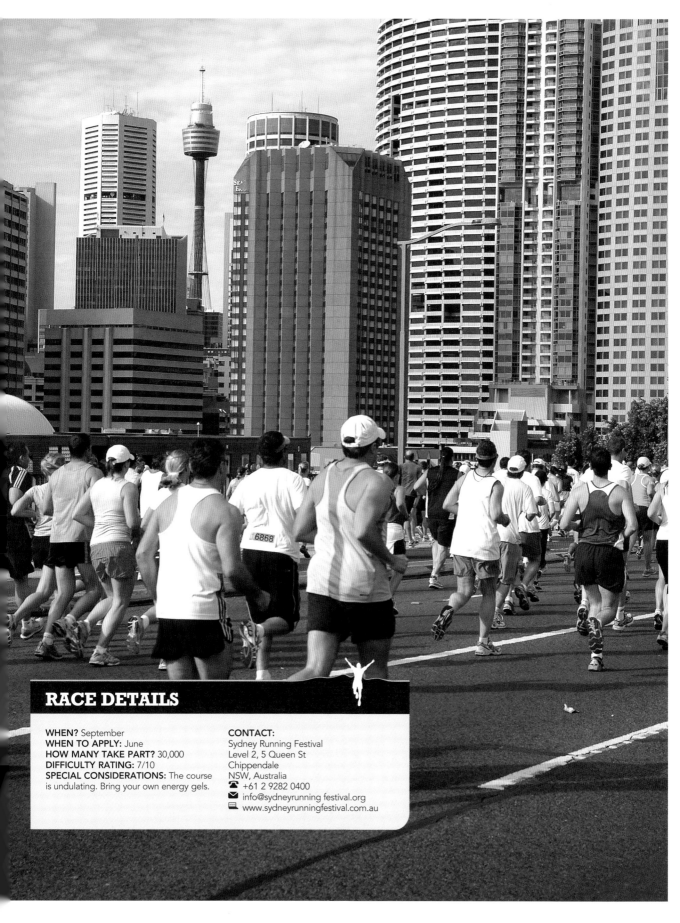

RACE DETAILS

WHEN? September
WHEN TO APPLY: June
HOW MANY TAKE PART? 30,000
DIFFICULTY RATING: 7/10
SPECIAL CONSIDERATIONS: The course
is undulating. Bring your own energy gels.

CONTACT:
Sydney Running Festival
Level 2, 5 Queen St
Chippendale
NSW, Australia
☎ +61 2 9282 0400
✉ info@sydneyrunning festival.org
🖥 www.sydneyrunningfestival.com.au

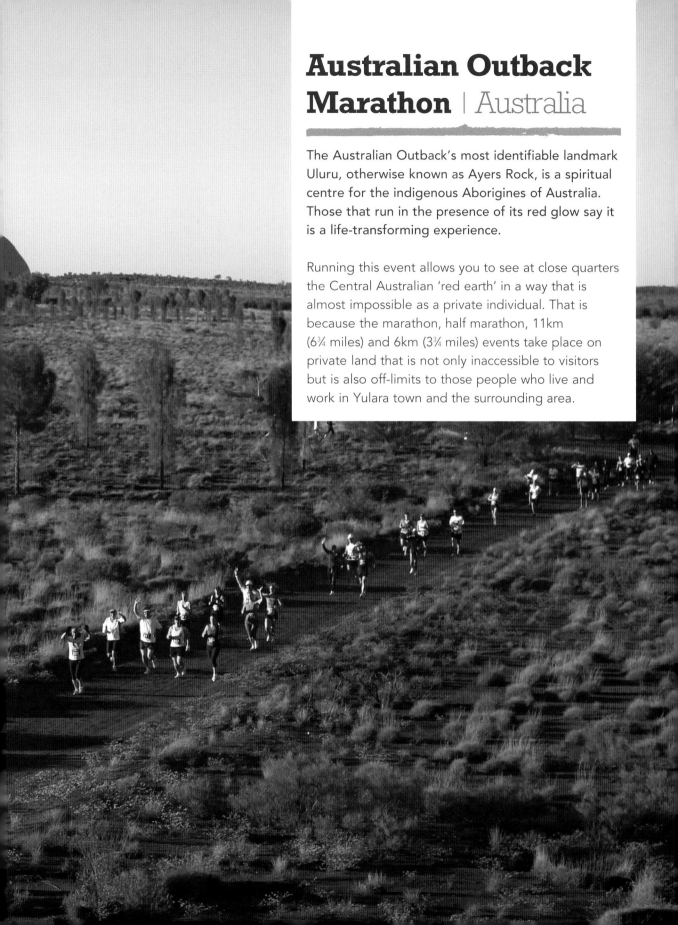

Australian Outback Marathon | Australia

The Australian Outback's most identifiable landmark Uluru, otherwise known as Ayers Rock, is a spiritual centre for the indigenous Aborigines of Australia. Those that run in the presence of its red glow say it is a life-transforming experience.

Running this event allows you to see at close quarters the Central Australian 'red earth' in a way that is almost impossible as a private individual. That is because the marathon, half marathon, 11km (6¾ miles) and 6km (3¾ miles) events take place on private land that is not only inaccessible to visitors but is also off-limits to those people who live and work in Yulara town and the surrounding area.

3

WHILE YOU'RE THERE

There is a **celebration dinner** as part of the marathon, held outdoors at a private site. Champagne and canapés are served upon arrival, and guests are serenaded by the marathon's own **didgeridoo player** while the sun sets over Uluru. By night find **an astronomer** onsite to point out the constellations as there is absolutely no atmospheric pollution to dim the glow of the night sky. See: www. australiasoutback.com.

The Australian Outback Marathon was conceived during a visit to Uluru in 2004 by two race visionaries, Mari-Mar and Michael Walton. Both were working on behalf of an agency called Travelling Fit. Not having been to Uluru before, they were in awe of the area and knew that it would be the perfect location for a running event. After several years of working on the idea, permissions were finally granted in 2008, and the Australian Outback Marathon was born.

The amazing landscape of Uluru and Kata Tjuta (a significant group of rock formations, locally called The Olgas) allows runners and spectators alike to appreciate views of these World Heritage-listed Sites from almost every part of the course. It is, however, only when you see these monolithic forms from a distance that you get a real sense of how large and majestic they are. With so few spectators along the course, runners get the feeling that they are at one with the spirit of the Australian Outback.

There are approximately 2km (1¼ miles) of sealed roads on the course as well as an additional 2km (1¼ miles) of unsealed but graded roads, and despite the dust and dirt the route generally offers a firm footing. As the area was once an ancient sea bed the course is flat; however there are a few sand dunes to navigate which enliven the run, and the views from the top are breathtaking.

Previous page: Spectacular countryside and a small field are two very appealing aspects of this course.

Above: Jogging in the 'red centre' as this part of the vast Outback is known, almost feels like you are on a different planet.

Right: The tracks and trails of the marathon course are made up of the famous red earth that surrounds the Ayers Rock Resort.

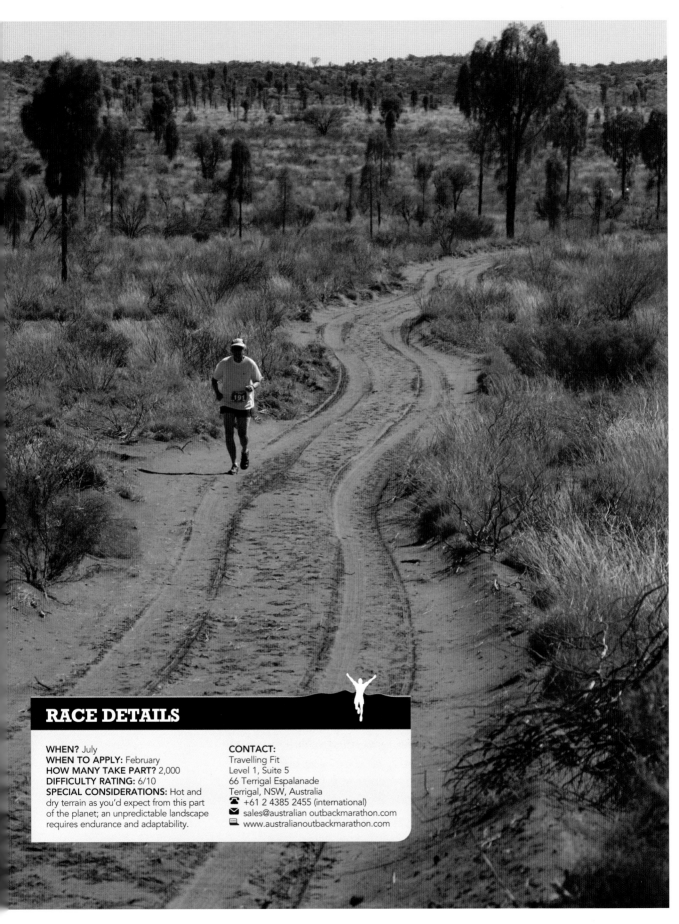

RACE DETAILS

WHEN? July
WHEN TO APPLY: February
HOW MANY TAKE PART? 2,000
DIFFICULTY RATING: 6/10
SPECIAL CONSIDERATIONS: Hot and dry terrain as you'd expect from this part of the planet; an unpredictable landscape requires endurance and adaptability.

CONTACT:
Travelling Fit
Level 1, Suite 5
66 Terrigal Espalanade
Terrigal, NSW, Australia
☎ +61 2 4385 2455 (international)
✉ sales@australian outbackmarathon.com
🖳 www.australianoutbackmarathon.com

Tokyo Marathon | Japan

Japan is one of the foremost countries of the world when it comes to marathons. The country's Olympic marathon record, from 1936 to the present, is second to none. The key to this has been an unrelenting concentration on elite performance. Marathons staged in Japan have traditionally been for restricted fields of a few dozen elite men or women with separate races for each on the championship model. Road space was freed up for these events by using a 'rolling closure' and if runners did not keep on schedule to finish in under 2½ or 3 hours, they were 'retired' into the sweep vehicle.

If you were an ordinary Japanese citizen and you wanted to take part in a marathon, your best chance was to jump on a plane and go to Honolulu, USA, to run in a race where the field was also mainly other Japanese runners. But that all changed with the advent of the first mass marathon in Japan, the 2007 Tokyo Marathon. Since 1981 Japanese marathons had subscribed to the elite model described above, but after minutely observing mass marathons in the rest of the world, and spending years planning their groundbreaking event, the Tokyo Marathon took the world by storm.

The 2007 race itself was a washout as it rained heavily for the duration. Yet such is the affinity the Japanese have for marathon running that it did not dampen their spirit. That first event was swamped by eager entrants, and now two or three times as many people apply for places as there are spaces. There is no indication that the Japanese love affair with marathon running is anywhere near over, as many of Japan's main cities have followed Tokyo's example and have converted their events to the popular model (among them Osaka, Kyoto, Nagoya, and Kobe).

It is the city's dedication to holding this event that defines the atmosphere – support is strong and public enthusiasm has always been there, even when the crowds at the roadside were encouraging national heroes rather than their nearest and dearest. Those who were not on the roadside were watching it on TV – Japan has the highest television-viewing figures for a marathon anywhere recorded.

WHILE YOU'RE THERE

Tokyo has the most populated landscape in the world, and its high-tech construction never fails to amaze.

Among the historic sites you should see are the **temples of Asakusa**, the **Imperial Palace** and the **Meiji Shrine**.

To get a grasp of this metropolis go to the top of the **Tokyo Metropolitan Government Building**, where you can benefit from a free view of the city. See: www.seejapan.co.uk

Right: Marathon running is a significant sport in Japan, where the events receive plenty of popular support.

RACE DETAILS

WHEN? February
WHEN TO APPLY: One year in advance
HOW MANY TAKE PART? 35,000
DIFFICULTY RATING: 4/10
SPECIAL CONSIDERATIONS: Fast and flat course which is surprisingly free of congestion. Be prepared for unpredictable weather and wind.

CONTACT:
KNT Tokyo Marathon Entry Desk
Kinki Nippon Tourist Co, Ltd (KNT)
Global Business Management Branch
Sumitomo-shoji kanda -Izumi-cho Bldg
12F,1–13 Kanda-Izumi-cho, Chiyoda-ku
Tokyo 101-0024, Japan
☎ +813 6891 9600
✉ tm2016@or.knt.co.jp
🖥 www.marathon.tokyo/en

The start gun is fired at the Tokyo Metropolitan Government Building, setting runners off on a downhill gradient towards the city's Yasukuni Shrine before taking a turn past the Imperial Palace and onward to Hibiya Park. Marathon day is the only time when these key landmarks are free of traffic, and that alone is worth celebrating. The distance from 11– 32km (7–20 miles) is relatively flat, but the test comes in the last quarter of the race, as runners must find the energy to ascend three bridges.

Runners come under their own steam from as many as 49 different countries to a race that less than ten years ago was by invitation only. Organisers want to see increasing international participation in the race, and it seems that they have many takers - all eager to experience the new developments in the world's most marathon-committed nation. Following the devastating earthquake and tsunami of 2011, future editions of the marathon will devote a percentage of profits to disaster relief.

Above: Shiba Park is a key landmark in the first section of the race and is generally well supported by the crowds.

Beijing Marathon | China

Just like the Chinese Tiger Economy itself, this sporting spectacle is evolving with the same rampant fervour. The Beijing Marathon has gone from a minority event to one that sparkles with the verve of a city happy to shout about itself.

In 1980 a national sports conference was held in Beijing at which it was decided to use sport to connect with the rest of the world. The Beijing Marathon was founded the following year as part of this outreach policy and marked the birth of the marathon in China. A total of 80 elite male runners were invited to participate in that first race, though they were almost lost in the immensity of the Tiananmen Square start and finish area. Women weren't accepted until 1989, the same year that amateur runners were first admitted. Participation has now reached 30,000, with the field divided between the marathon, a half marathon and a fun run.

The start and finish were moved from Tiananmen Square to the Workers' Stadium for many years, though the start is now back in Tiananmen Square, just as it was for the 2008 Olympic Games. Apart from the first few kilometres, the city marathon course is quite different to the Olympic one.

WHILE YOU'RE THERE

October is one of the best times to visit the city of Beijing and there is always a packed arts programme at the **National Theatre**.

It is also the season to see the lotus flower in full glory, as well as the rich reds of the maple leaf. There is even a Maple Leaf Festival in the western reaches of Beijing at **Xiangshan**.

For some night-time revelry the best nightlife spots are **Houhai Bar Street**, and Sanlitun Bar Street.

Left: Beijing puts on a spectacle for the world to watch on marathon day.

From Tiananmen Square, the world's largest city-centre square which can hold up to a million people, runners file past the Great Hall of the People, the Monument to the People's Heroes, the Chairman Mao Memorial Hall, and the gate to the Imperial Palace, or 'Forbidden City'. This impressive grouping of sights is all in the first few hundred metres, then followed by long, straight sections without much to see as the route loops through the western side of town.

Below: Tiananmen Square is synonymous with the imagery of China. It is here, in front of the portrait of Chairman Mao, where the marathon gets underway.

The National Museum of China and Zhongshan Park are the most prominent landmarks until the runners reach the 2008 Olympic Stadium known to the world as The Bird's Nest, with the Olympic Aquatic Centre alongside it.

The Marathon is held every year on the third Sunday in October during Beijing's golden autumn when it is dry and cool, and the city is at its very best.

RACE DETAILS

WHEN? October
WHEN TO APPLY: By July
HOW MANY TAKE PART? 30,000
DIFFICULTY RATING: 5/10
SPECIAL CONSIDERATIONS: It is a race you run for the experience, not the scenery. Tiananmen Square is subject to tight security, so try and arrive one hour before the start time. Traffic can be difficult.

CONTACT:
✉ overseas@beijing-marathon.com
🖥 www.beijing-marathon.com

The Great Wall Marathon | China

If running a marathon isn't a big enough test, then try doing it along the Great Wall of China. Taking on the 5,164 steps of this world-famous structure is one of the biggest challenges a runner can face.

Many have called the Great Wall Marathon the hardest marathon in the world. But the race is equally one of the most picturesque, offering the thrill of competing on top of one the world's great landmarks.

Built on a mountain range, the wall rises and drops dramatically and offers consistently superb views. The section of the route run along the wall is 3.5km (just over 2 miles) long, with the rest on asphalt roads through nearby villages.

RACE DETAILS

WHEN? May
WHEN TO APPLY: A year in advance due to small capacity
HOW MANY TAKE PART? 2,000
DIFFICULTY RATING: 8/10
SPECIAL CONSIDERATIONS: Supreme stamina required as you don't just run past the wall, but also run up it. Plenty of water is provided. Bring your own gels, if you want them.

CONTACT:
The Great Wall Marathon
Albatros Adventure
Tondergade 16
DK-1752 Copenhagen V
Denmark
☎ +45 36 98 9 8 99
✉ marathon@albatros-travel.com
🖥 www.great-wall-marathon.com

⑥

WHILE YOU'RE THERE

The engineering feat of the Great Wall is worth another look after the run. One of the best spots to see it is at **Mutianyu**, which is less crowded, and surrounded by greenery. The wall stretches through the spectacular wildlife habitats, offering the lucky few an opportunity to spot the **Siberian tiger**, the **giant panda**, **black bears**, and the **Sitka deer**, which all live along the length of the wall. See: www.cnto.org.uk

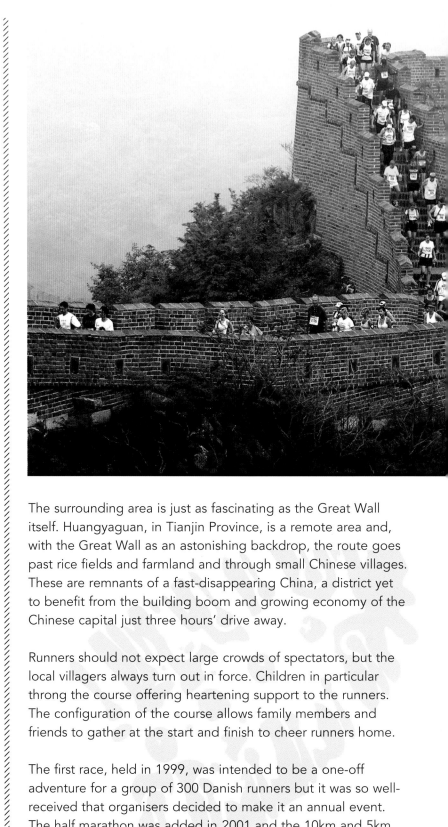

The surrounding area is just as fascinating as the Great Wall itself. Huangyaguan, in Tianjin Province, is a remote area and, with the Great Wall as an astonishing backdrop, the route goes past rice fields and farmland and through small Chinese villages. These are remnants of a fast-disappearing China, a district yet to benefit from the building boom and growing economy of the Chinese capital just three hours' drive away.

Runners should not expect large crowds of spectators, but the local villagers always turn out in force. Children in particular throng the course offering heartening support to the runners. The configuration of the course allows family members and friends to gather at the start and finish to cheer runners home.

The first race, held in 1999, was intended to be a one-off adventure for a group of 300 Danish runners but it was so well-received that organisers decided to make it an annual event. The half marathon was added in 2001 and the 10km and 5km

Previous page: Running on the Great Wall is one of life's incredible experiences.

Above: The Great Wall is the width of a marching army in places, but the surface is uneven and sloping in all directions, and this adds to the difficulty of the race.

Top right: The Great Wall Marathon is an endurance test at altitude as much as a marathon and is not for the faint-hearted.

Above right: Dirt tracks make up more than half of the terrain of the marathon and are usually lined with local well-wishers.

distances in 2004. Numbers have grown steadily from just under 100 runners in 2000 to more than 1,700 10 years later. Logistics in such a remote area and the need to limit numbers on the wall itself make it likely that organisers will cap the field at 2,000. Temperatures are usually around 20–25°C (68–77°F), but there have been years when they have reached 35°C (95°F). A low of 16°C (61°F) was recorded in 2008. Rain is unusual at the time of the race.

The steps on the Great Wall are the major challenge, especially as they are steep, irregular and uneven. The rest of the route is also testing, as the gravel and dirt roads wind through hilly farmland and villages. This marathon is not one for fast times, and runners would not want to spend much time looking at their watch when there is so much else around to take in. This run offers a unique and life-enhancing experience which is not available from more conventional organised tours to visit the Great Wall.

Ladakh Marathon | India

WHILE YOU'RE THERE

Although running is a relatively new venture in the area, Ladakh is a hub for **adventure tourism**. Trekking, mountaineering, river rafting and cycling are all popular hobbies for those traveling to northern India. Situated at the borders of Pakistan, India and China, Ladakh remains a geopolitically strategic trade location and tourists may visit several museums in the main town of Leh. The Tibetan Markets in Leh are well worth an extended browse. The Indus valley near Leh and the Nubra Valley offer a **breathtaking view** of the mountains. For marathon, half and 7km (4¾ mile) runners, a trip to the summit of the Khardung-La pass is well worth it.

Right: Khardung-La runners descend from the pass, where they reached an altitude of 5,370m (17,617ft) on the highest motorable civilian road in the world.

Situated in the far north of India, Ladakh is where the high Himalaya meets the western extreme of the Tibetan plateau. Average elevation exceeds 3,000m (10,000ft) and the highest point is the Saser Kangri massif of the east Karakorum, which rises to over 7,600m (25,000ft). Mountains to the south and southwest of Ladakh cut off the rain-bearing monsoon clouds: barring freak weather, Ladakh is a high-altitude cold desert. The air is dry and summers are pleasant to hot. Winters are cold.

Ladakh occupies a geo-politically strategic position where the borders of Pakistan, India and China meet. Besides being a tourist destination, the main town, Leh, is also a major military base. Ladakh has one of the lowest population densities in India, making it a welcome contrast to the crowding and congestion elsewhere in the sub-continent. It is a hub for adventure tourism: people come for trekking, mountaineering, river rafting, cycling – and, of late, for running.

The Ladakh Marathon is organised by Rimo Expeditions, which is among India's biggest outdoor companies. The Marathon title includes three other associated events - a 7km (4¾ mile) run, a half marathon and a 72km (45 mile) ultra-marathon over the 5,370m (17,617ft) high Khardung-La pass, the highest motorable civilian road in the world. Steadily growing numbers testify to the success of the event: from 1,500 runners in the first year, participation has now risen to 4,000.

The Khardung-La Challenge (as the ultra is called) has also increased numbers: from 11 initially to almost 90 in 2015. The Challenge straddles two sides of the mountain bordering Leh to the north. It starts in Khardung village at an altitude of 4,000m (13,100ft). Runners climb the pass through North Pullu (4,700m/15,500ft) to the summit of the Khardung-La pass before descending to South Pullu (4,600m/15,300ft) and concluding their 72km (45 mile) epic at the Ladakh Public School in Leh at 3,400m (11,200ft). The overwhelming sensation of the Challenge is losing oneself in the vast mountainous landscape.

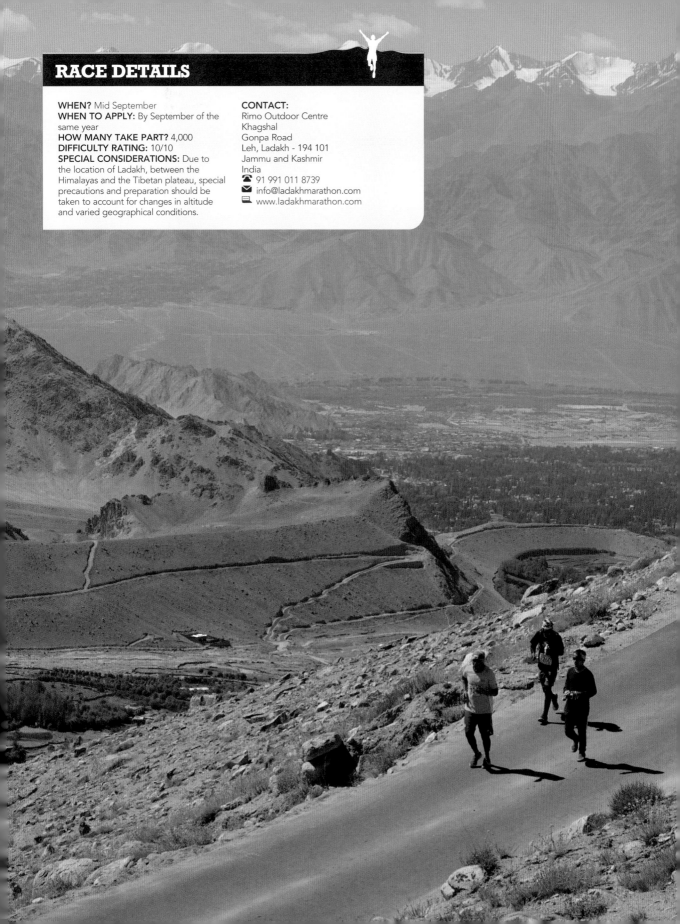

RACE DETAILS

WHEN? Mid September
WHEN TO APPLY: By September of the same year
HOW MANY TAKE PART? 4,000
DIFFICULTY RATING: 10/10
SPECIAL CONSIDERATIONS: Due to the location of Ladakh, between the Himalayas and the Tibetan plateau, special precautions and preparation should be taken to account for changes in altitude and varied geographical conditions.

CONTACT:
Rimo Outdoor Centre
Khagshal
Gonpa Road
Leh, Ladakh - 194 101
Jammu and Kashmir
India
☎ 91 991 011 8739
✉ info@ladakhmarathon.com
🖥 www.ladakhmarathon.com

The full marathon, half marathon and the 7km (4¾ mile) are all run on the south side of the mountain, in and around Leh. The Indus River is the main geographical feature common to the three events. The Ladakh Marathon encompasses all of Leh's varied geography from its high mountain pass to its famous river. The full marathon starts at Shanti Stupa (3,600m/11,800ft) overlooking Leh. Runners descend to the 'lowlands' (relatively speaking) of the Indus and cross the river twice (near Markalak and at Choglamsar) and eventually climb back up to finish at the Ladakh Public School. The half marathon begins at Shanti Stupa but stays to the north side of the Indus to reach the common finish by a shorter route.

Local runners have dominated the Ladakh Marathon since it started up in 2012. At the 2015 race Katharina Leuthner from Austria finished third, the highest placed non-Ladakhi, and said: 'This is the toughest race I have run so far'.

Organising the Ladakh Marathon is complicated because everything from small bottles of water to T-shirts have to be trucked or airlifted into Leh from lowland India. Medical assistance is crucial. Leh lies at such altitude that all outsiders running here are coming from lower elevations. For the 2015 race, organisers requisitioned 14 ambulances. The military also made its medical teams available. As part of the race's community involvement programme, some of the aid stations en route are operated by the villages the race passes through, which lends a distinctive local flavour to the event.

The aid stations for the Khardung-La Challenge were the responsibility of Kyagar in the Nubra valley, race founder Motup's home village. Apart from the stupendous physical landscape along its route, the charm of the Ladakh Marathon lies in it being the fulfilment of the personal dream of someone born and raised in that same landscape.

Left: Marathon runners head upstream near the Indus with the Spituk monastery receding in the background.

Siberian International Marathon | Russia

In this part of western Siberia this race is awaited with the same anticipation as a national holiday. So closely does the marathon touch the Siberian soul that a statue 'The Flying Marathoner' was erected in the heart of the city as a reminder to those who might otherwise miss the event. Come race day it is adorned with the names of the participants who have come to run.

As soon as the city of Omsk opened its doors to visitors in 1990, an international marathon was organised to mark this historic event. More than 40 nationalities come from far-flung corners of the globe to take part each year and are greeted with open arms. It is something locals look forward to, and during the build-up advertisements abound with the marathon logos. The city's media approach a frenzy in their constant chatter about the race events. All this builds excitement and anticipation. On race day the full cross-section of Omsk society turns out in force: students, politicians and pensioners.

With the most 'continental' of climates – being several thousand kilometres from the nearest ocean – Omsk is bone-chillingly cold in winter, but on race day basks in the early August sunshine. At the start in 2012 - timed to coincide with the men's Olympic Marathon in London - the temperature was 36°C (97°F). This resulted in the race date being shifted to mid-September, but after a few chilly editions, the organisers decided to move back to the early August date. Before the 2012 race the average temperature on marathon day had been 22°-25°C (71°-77°F).

The start is heralded by church bells ringing at the 17th-century Cathedral of the Assumption, outside which the race begins and ends. The first part of the course takes runners through the 19th-century part of town, built at a time when the Tsarist Empire was still consolidating its grip on its sub-Asiatic hinterland. Runners run out and back along the birch-lined embankments of the impressively broad Irtysh River. The second half of the course runs through the industrial part of the city, including the largest oil refinery in Russia.

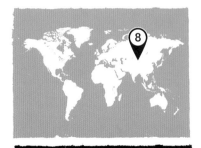

WHILE YOU'RE THERE

The city centre around **Lyubinsky Prospekt** is best explored on foot, as the stomping ground of Russia's great literary giant Dostoevsky. The historical part of town is centred here, near the **Om** and **Irtysh Rivers**. It is lined with century-old buildings of former merchant salons, **grand residences and churches**. Omsk was a centre for the Trans-Siberian Railway, which brought great affluence in the early 20th century.

Right: The Siberian Marathon takes place at the start of a week of national festivities and is well supported by local people in the city.

Spectators who don't find viewing space at the start have plenty of opportunity to intercept the runners at other points along the course. People turn out in force to support runners in all possible ways – only in Omsk will you be offered cranberry water and homemade pies as you run.

The closing ceremony is treated as seriously as at the Olympic Games. Russian sports journalist Boris Prokopiev, making a direct comparison, described it as 'bright, colourful, gorgeous; a sports performance lasting hours and incorporating effects like waterfalls of balloons and fireworks as the athletes stand proudly on the rostrum'.

RACE DETAILS

WHEN? August
WHEN TO APPLY: December of the year before
HOW MANY TAKE PART? 1,300
DIFFICULTY RATING: 7/10
SPECIAL CONSIDERATIONS: The weather is likely to be extreme and can sometimes hit 35–40°C (95–104°F). A largely flat course on asphalt.

CONTACT:
Siberian International Marathon
Non-Profit-Making Partnership "Marathon"
Pevtsova ul, 1
Omsk, 644043, Russia
☎ +7 (3812) 242 567
✉ mail@runsim.ru
🖥 www.runsim.ru

Mumbai Marathon | India

WHILE YOU'RE THERE
Just a day in the congested city
might leave you wanting to
escape to find some fresher air.
Take a ferry near the **Gate of
India** landmark to **Elephant
Island** to see ancient temples
carved into caves.
One of the best treats you can
give yourself after the marathon
is to take afternoon tea at the
Leela Hotel (www.theleela.
com) one of India's most
affordable lavish hotels.
Or if you have more than a few
days to spare, take the train to
sunny **Goa**, and enjoy its many
beaches.

Right: Helicopters are used to capture
footage that is shown around the world.

Far right: This is a marathon with plenty of
views to occupy the runner's attention.

The Mumbai Marathon was born with a bang in 2004, and launched with all the razzamatazz you would expect of a Bollywood blockbuster. Hyped in the newspapers daily for the preceding month, street billboards bellowed the message and a laser show projected images onto the side of the Air India building on Marine Drive, visible to all for miles around. Would this fledgling event collapse under the weight of its own expectation, especially as Indian participants were nowhere to be seen?

But the Mumbai Marathon is a festival and a celebration – it may be spearheaded by top-class international runners, but everyone wants a piece of the action. The organisers appreciated this from the start, knowing that there was no room for half measures, and fought a long, hard battle with sometimes reluctant officials to clear a space for the marathon on Mumbai's crowded streets. With some visionary help from people in high places, the show got on the road after only one year of preparing the ground.

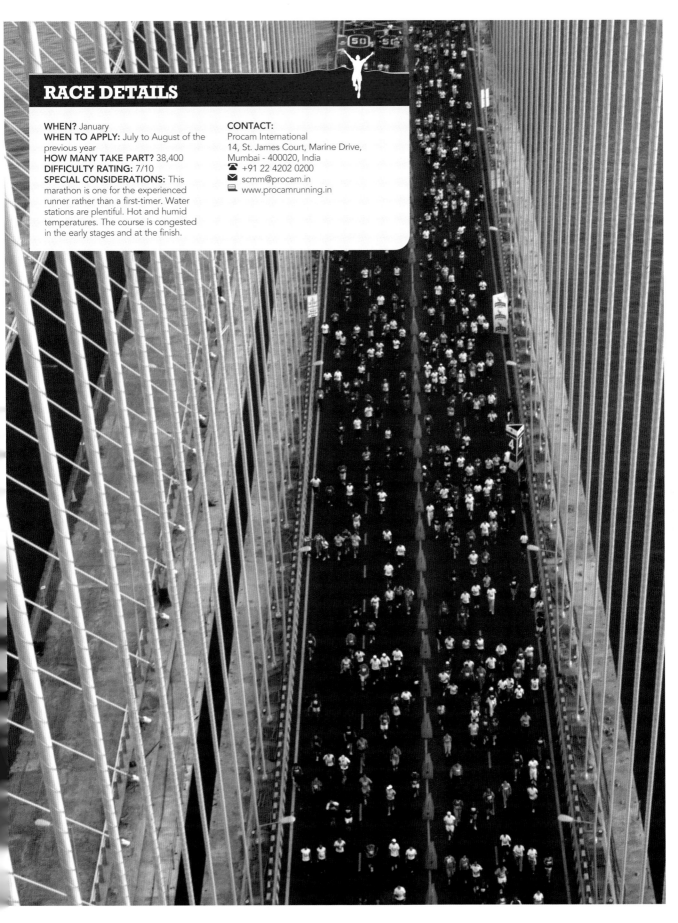

RACE DETAILS

WHEN? January
WHEN TO APPLY: July to August of the previous year
HOW MANY TAKE PART? 38,400
DIFFICULTY RATING: 7/10
SPECIAL CONSIDERATIONS: This marathon is one for the experienced runner rather than a first-timer. Water stations are plentiful. Hot and humid temperatures. The course is congested in the early stages and at the finish.

CONTACT:
Procam International
14, St. James Court, Marine Drive,
Mumbai - 400020, India
☎ +91 22 4202 0200
✉ scmm@procam.in
🖥 www.procamrunning.in

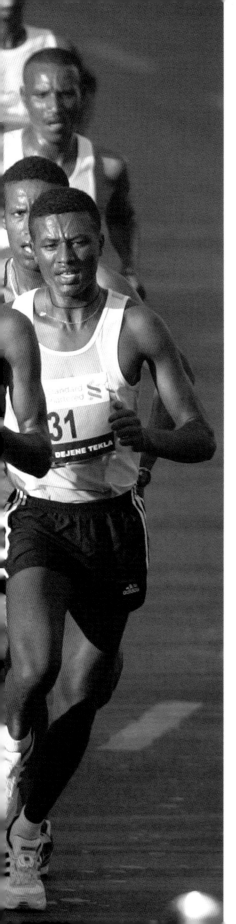

Mumbai permanently buzzes with swarms of cars, trucks, taxis and bikes, with the occasional cow weaving its way through the urban mayhem. That is just on a quiet day. Marathon day brings a completely different feel as the roads are cleared to make way for a spectacle that brings this city together. Everyone, from Bollywood stars and heavyweight corporate players to juice wallahs and street urchins, are either watching or taking part in a display of solidarity for an international event that is beamed across the world.

Never was this more in evidence than on 18 January 2009, when the race went ahead just seven weeks after the terrorist attacks that attempted to cripple the city. The marathon was a statement of the collective will of its citizens, expressing both their strong spirit and their resolve.

As a runner you'll be swept up in the tide of race fever come the day. More than 1,000 volunteers, private security guards and 800 police secure the course, which goes out and back, taking in a loop of Mumbai's new addition to the urban landscape – the 4km (2½ mile) Bandra-Worli Sealink, which although devoid of spectators offers impressive panoramas of the city.

Largely because of the Mumbai Marathon, running has become fashionable among the Bollywood set and this is reflected in the aspirational demographic among the tens of thousands of entrants in the marathon (4,000), half marathon (14,000) and 6km (3¾ miles) 'Dream Run' (25,000). This is all despite the climate, which is not conducive to fast running, although the heat is offset somewhat by the early 5.40am marathon start.

Invited elite runners have recorded surprisingly fast times – men under 2:10 and women 2:25. Indian athletes habitually run their fastest times in the race, spurred on by the occasion and the illustrious competition.

The Mumbai Marathon with its inclusive and international spirit is not just a race, but a vision of a new India.

Left: The elite runners in any marathon field are a sight to behold.

RACE DETAILS

WHEN? February
WHEN TO APPLY: June of the year before
HOW MANY TAKE PART? 5,000
DIFFICULTY RATING: 8/10
SPECIAL CONSIDERATIONS: There are long stretches of uphill running. Things can get hot, humid and dusty, often reaching more than 30°C (86°F), but there is plenty of shade as well as water stations. Traffic and exhaust fumes can be an issue.

CONTACT:
Wild Frontiers (Pty) Ltd
PO Box 844
Halfway House 1685
South Africa
☎ +27 011 702 2035
✉ reservations@wildfrontiers.com
🖳 www.kilimanjaromarathon.com

Kilimanjaro
Marathon | Tanzania

Climbing Mount Kilimanjaro features on more than a few people's ultimate 'wish list' of things to do before they die. Running the Kilimanjaro Marathon provides a taste of the same adventure, taking the runner up as far as the lower slopes of the world's highest 'free-standing' mountain.

Mount Kilimanjaro, at just short of 6,000m (19,700ft) is Africa's highest mountain. Glaciers flow down from the summit, and the sheer presence of this huge mountain dominates the northern part of Tanzania for miles around. An icon in Africa, 'Kili' as she is affectionately known, is one of the sights everyone should see at least once at close range.

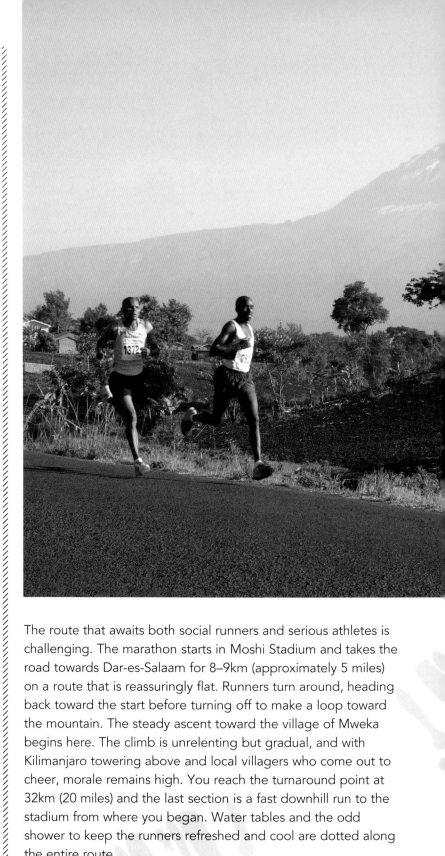

The route that awaits both social runners and serious athletes is challenging. The marathon starts in Moshi Stadium and takes the road towards Dar-es-Salaam for 8–9km (approximately 5 miles) on a route that is reassuringly flat. Runners turn around, heading back toward the start before turning off to make a loop toward the mountain. The steady ascent toward the village of Mweka begins here. The climb is unrelenting but gradual, and with Kilimanjaro towering above and local villagers who come out to cheer, morale remains high. You reach the turnaround point at 32km (20 miles) and the last section is a fast downhill run to the stadium from where you began. Water tables and the odd shower to keep the runners refreshed and cool are dotted along the entire route.

Previous page: The start of the race is well supported with a party atmosphere as the athletes ready themselves for the course ahead.

Above: As its growing popularity attests, running a marathon under the watchful eye of Mount Kilimanjaro is an experience that any runner will treasure.

Right: This marathon field is relatively small but well supported.

The scenery encapsulates Africa's traditional landscape and local life. It passes many smallholder farms, villages, and banana and coffee plantations, as well as patches of forest. You get a real flavour of Africa as you run past the markets, shops and shebeens of Moshi. Local children often run alongside, holding your hand as they cheer you on. The race provides a source of great excitement to the residents who give ample vocal support. It is their presence, as much as that of the awe-inspiring mountain, that remains etched on the memory.

Kilimanjaro Marathon started as a small affair with only 500 runners, many of them foreign, but has grown to involve over 5,000 locals and foreigners in the marathon, half marathon and fun run.

Safaricom Marathon | Kenya

Transplanting a marathon race into a safari park is an unmistakably Western idea, although nonetheless interesting for that. The race was founded in 2000 when there was nothing else like it anywhere on the continent. Safaricom, the region's telecom provider, has helped to drum up foreign interest in running in Africa and has used the marathon as a vehicle to improve awareness of living conditions for the local people. Since the inaugural race, more than US$3 million has been generated for wildlife conservation, community development, health and education projects all over Kenya.

The event takes in spectacular scenery – Mount Kenya lies to the south of the Lewa Wildlife Conservancy, the site of the run, and there are breathtaking views north toward Samburu National Reserve and Mount Ololokwe. The course is challenging with no asphalt in sight. It is all on dirt roads that form an undulating 21km (13 miles) lap within the reserve, across the open savannah, along riverbanks and through acacia woodland before finishing close to Lewa's Park headquarters. Half-marathon runners do one lap of the course, full marathon runners two.

The heavily protected 26,000-hectare (65,000-acre) wildlife sanctuary is home to more than 100 rhino, herds of elephant and a vast assortment of plains game including zebra, giraffe, and buffalo, so you will never be far away from the wildlife. The thrill of running this race is that you are on the animals' territory. A large and experienced team of armed rangers watch over the route, with two helicopters and a spotter plane in the air throughout the race. Water stations and first aid points are situated every 2.5km (1½ miles) along the course. Medical support at the finish is provided by the African Medical Research Foundation (AMREF) and its Flying Doctor Service, the Kenya Red Cross, as well as local hospitals.

Spectators have access to the route at certain points and the understandable restrictions make support all the more appreciated and effective for the runners. Apart from these few points, runners sample the scenery in what must appear to

WHILE YOU'RE THERE

Just like its marathon, the abundance of activities on offer around Lewa centres around wildlife. The **Lewa Wildlife Conservancy** offers trips where visitors can indulge in the abundant nature. There are a selection of **safaris** that will take you close to leopards, cheetahs, lions, rhino and elephants. You can also take part in a **bush walk**, where you can stroll among flora and fauna.

Above right: It is not uncommon to see the wildlife at very close range in this marathon.

Right: The marathon runs directly through the habitat of zebras, elephants, and giraffes, and so novel precautions are requisite.

be a vast wilderness away from civilization. Most runners and spectators spend the night before and after the race in Lewa in specially erected campsites within the conservation area. This gives the runners a chance to camp in the African bush and to see wildlife throughout the weekend.

The weather at the end of June, when the run is staged, is hot with temperatures at midday around 30°C (86°F). Mornings and evenings are cool with a strong breeze coming off the mountain. In addition, the race is run at an altitude of 1,700m (5,580ft) and this will have a definite restraining effect on the runners' pace.

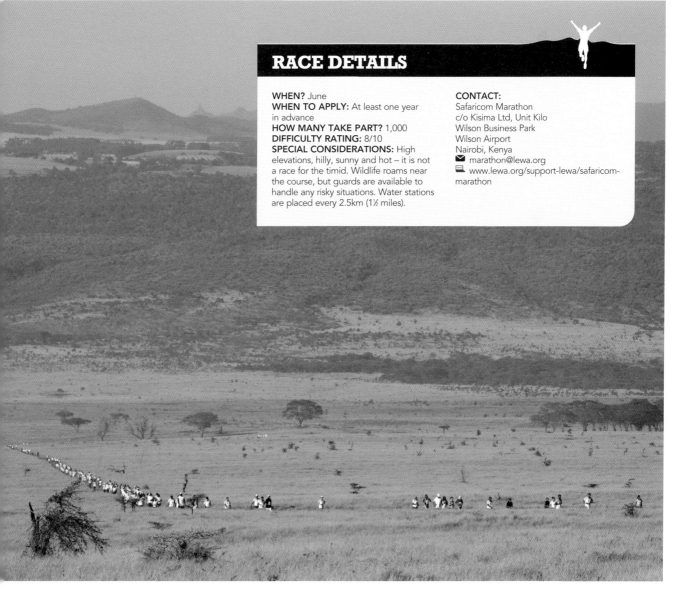

RACE DETAILS

WHEN? June
WHEN TO APPLY: At least one year in advance
HOW MANY TAKE PART? 1,000
DIFFICULTY RATING: 8/10
SPECIAL CONSIDERATIONS: High elevations, hilly, sunny and hot – it is not a race for the timid. Wildlife roams near the course, but guards are available to handle any risky situations. Water stations are placed every 2.5km (1½ miles).

CONTACT:
Safaricom Marathon
c/o Kisima Ltd, Unit Kilo
Wilson Business Park
Wilson Airport
Nairobi, Kenya
✉ marathon@lewa.org
🖥 www.lewa.org/support-lewa/safaricom-marathon

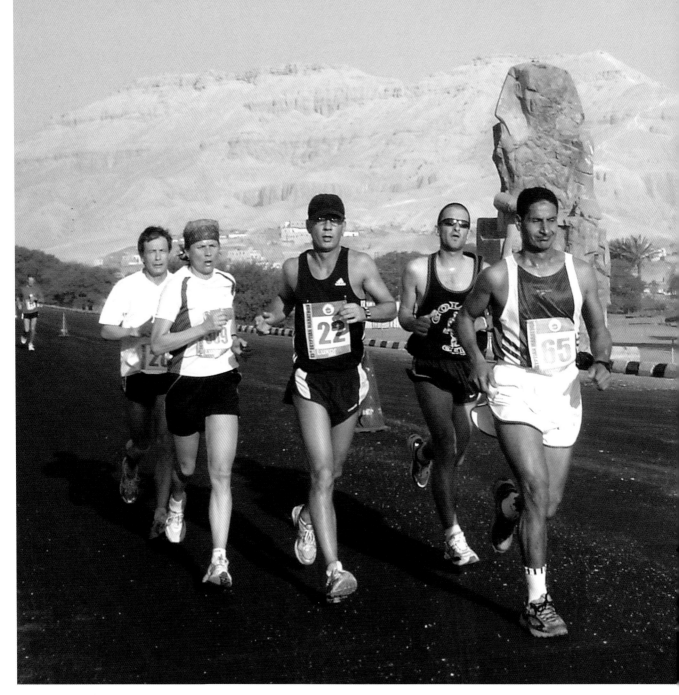

RACE DETAILS

WHEN? January
WHEN TO APPLY: June of the year before
HOW MANY TAKE PART? 1,500
DIFFICULTY RATING: 7/10
SPECIAL CONSIDERATIONS: The course can get congested and invaded by children asking for money.

CONTACT: Event Sports
1/4 Anwar El-Mofty St. (Area No.1)
Nasr City,
Cairo, Egypt
☎ +202 2260 69 30
✉ info@egyptianmarathon.net
🖥 www.egyptianmarathon.com

Egyptian Marathon | Egypt

Running in Egypt is an activity that is as old as the Pyramids: King Taharka, who reigned between 690 and 665BC established a 100km (62 mile)-race for his army. There is still a 100km (62 mile) Pharonic Race as well as the Egyptian Marathon itself, using the now standard marathon distance of 42.2km (26 miles 385 yards).

Luxor, the host city, offers mild to warm conditions in late January when the run is scheduled, at a time when most of the Northern Hemisphere is suffering the chills of winter. The first event on the itinerary is a 3.4km (2 mile) warm-up 'breakfast run' starting at Luxor Temple and finishing at Karnak Temple, a massive complex that was the centre of Theban civilization, and evolved over 2,000 years. The participants keep the spirit of the past alive and it is common to see them running in various Egyptian regalia, from Pharoaonic costume to Cleopatra-style outfits.

The more serious racing starts the following day on the west bank of the Nile at 7.30am, and with luck there will be a cool breeze wafting across the desert landscape. The race starts and finishes against the spectacular backdrop of Queen Hatshepsut's tomb, also justifiably known as the Splendour of Splendours.

The four-lap route takes you to the entrance of the world-famous Valley of the Kings, which counts Tutankhamun's burial site among the many Pharaohs entombed here. In benign conditions, the first couple of laps on the wide and well-surfaced roads mean that the run can be appreciated as a tour of an extraordinary outdoor museum. You pass the Temple of Ramses III and later the Colossi of Memnon. Beyond, there lies the timeless Egyptian countryside, with swathes of sugar cane, alfalfa and date palms, creating a scene straight from a papyrus frieze, with runners as the focus of the composition.

WHILE YOU'RE THERE

You don't have to go far to find some of the most awe-inspiring ancient temples on the planet once you're in the area, with the **Valley of the Kings** being a definite highlight.

There are three main areas to focus on once you're in town: the busy city centre, the north-easterly village of **Karnak**, and also the many ancient remains of **Thebes**, located on the West Bank of the world-famous River Nile. By night there is a guided light show around the relics. See: www.exodustravel.co.uk

SAFETY WARNING

Always check your government's travel safety recommendations when considering travel to less stable regions.

Left: Running the Egyptian Marathon is like running through history, with ancient landmarks continually coming into view.

'White Nights' Marathon | Russia

The name of the run is derived from the 'white nights' that this part of Northern Russia experiences in the height of summer. Almost 24 hours of sun lends a mysterious twilight to what many people call the country's most beautiful city – St Petersburg, or Petersburg to which it is more commonly referred. To run here provides an experience that is one of a kind.

Part of the challenge, however, is finding the essential information necessary to start in the first place. The race is not as well established as other events staged in major world cities and doesn't provide the same facilities that international runners might expect. So far, there are no official tour operators for the event, or even an online registration option. For many that come to run here, the absence of a slick administration is part of the charm, giving the same kind of rawness of spirit that old-style marathons had – but located in a major city.

Below: The White Nights Marathon was celebrated as part of the St Petersburg's tri-centennial celebrations in 2003 and featured other fun runs.

RACE DETAILS

WHEN? Late June
WHEN TO APPLY: By January of the same year
HOW MANY TAKE PART? 1,100
DIFFICULTY RATING: 5/10
SPECIAL CONSIDERATIONS: The organisation and set-up is less slick than other world marathons. Advice and assistance is low on the ground. Prepare well in advance.

CONTACT:
White Nights Marathon
Office 11/2, Nevsky pr.32
St. Petersburg
Russia
☎ +812 312 90 15
✉ info@wnmarathon.ru
🖥 www.wnmarathon.ru

Those that make it here will discover Russia's greatest city awaiting them in all its glory. The fast marathon course follows river embankments and takes in historic landmarks such as the world-famous Hermitage museum, fabulous architecture, green spaces and even the main shopping area. The start and finish takes place in the Palace Square.

Petersburg is young by European standards, founded just 300 years ago by Tsar Peter the Great. It became the Russian capital in 1712. The 300-day siege of Leningrad (as the city was known from 1924–91) occurred here during World War II when almost three million civilians refused to surrender to their enemy, despite the hardships of famine and the bitter cold.

This marathon demands stoicism, but many find the challenge intensifies the experience. Rye bread, bananas and bottled water are handed out at regularly positioned drink stations. If you want new-fangled sports drinks and gels, it is better to come prepared. Instead of clocks, you'll find there are strategically placed officials on hand to shout out your time.

Istanbul Marathon | Turkey

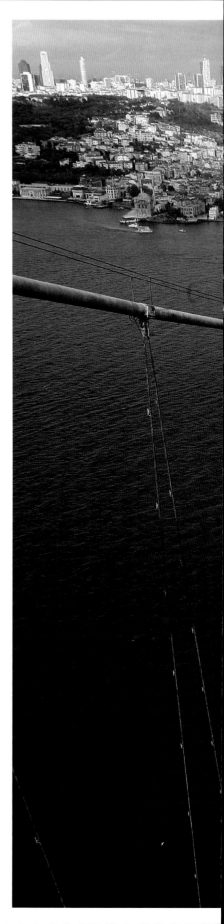

Istanbul is where Asia meets Europe. Its exclusive position provides the city with a unique selling point: this is the only race in the world in which you cross between two continents.

The incentive to stage a marathon here originally came from a sizeable group of German runners who, after running a Nile marathon, were looking for similar opportunities elsewhere. They provided 34 of the runners in that first event in 1979. Not many races are set up to serve a small group of interested foreign runners, but Istanbul's position as a continental crossing point meant that it could capitalise on the interest that foreign runners still continue to show in running in its symbolic location.

Runners complete only a token few hundred metres in Asia, as the race launches itself into Europe from the toll plaza on the Asian side of the Bosphorus Bridge. After the up-slope of the bridge, on the European side you drop down sharply, losing 90m (295 ft) before reaching the Bosphorus after 5km (3 miles). Thereafter the course is nearly all flat until the final kilometre.

The course offers a combination of historic and scenic settings between the continents and the three strategic and historic waterways of the Bosphorus, the Golden Horn and the Sea of Marmara. At the same time, the run takes a tour of more than 3,000 years of historical landmarks, during which three empires rose and fell.

Along the Bosphorus, giant Russian ships glide silently past, startlingly close, on their way from the Black Sea to the Mediterranean. On shore, the course takes you past the old and the new – from the 15th-century Rumelihisari fortress to the modern-day Galatasaray football stadium. After 10km (6 miles) you pass below the 62m (203ft)-high medieval stone Galata Tower, a Christian relic from pre-Ottoman times, before crossing the Galata Bridge over the Golden Horn.

Right: The Bosphorus Bridge represents the crossing point from Asia to Europe.

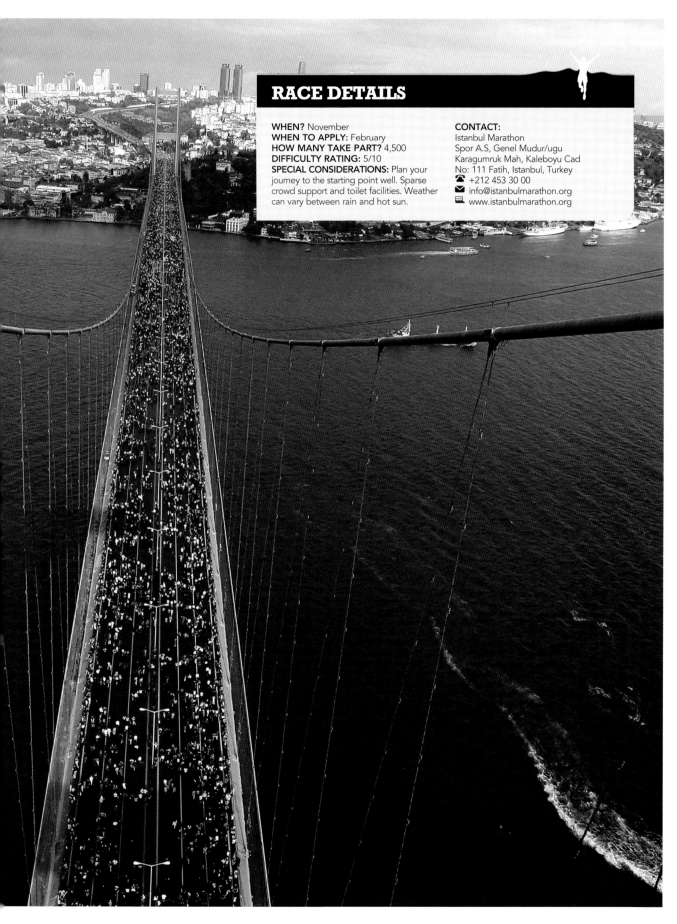

RACE DETAILS

WHEN? November
WHEN TO APPLY: February
HOW MANY TAKE PART? 4,500
DIFFICULTY RATING: 5/10
SPECIAL CONSIDERATIONS: Plan your journey to the starting point well. Sparse crowd support and toilet facilities. Weather can vary between rain and hot sun.

CONTACT:
Istanbul Marathon
Spor A.S, Genel Mudur/ugu
Karagumruk Mah, Kaleboyu Cad
No: 111 Fatih, Istanbul, Turkey
☎ +212 453 30 00
✉ info@istanbulmarathon.org
🖳 www.istanbulmarathon.org

14

WHILE YOU'RE THERE

This atmospheric city will always occupy your senses. When sightseeing check opening hours, places have random opening times. The **Sultanahmet Topkapi Palace** is best visited early in the morning when there are fewer crowds. Be sure to check out the fourth courtyard and the (no longer operational) harem, which many miss. The **Blue Mosque** is worth a visit at night when there is always a sound and light show. By night the side streets around **Istiklal Street** boast lots of nightlife; chic café bars, bistros, restaurants, nightclubs and music clubs such as Club 360. See: www.gototurkey.co.uk

The course then travels 7km (4½ miles) along the west bank of the historic waterway before cutting across the only landward side of town to reach the Sea of Marmara.

From 20–40km (12½–25 miles) runners go out and back to the west, returning around the seaward side of the 15th-century Topkapi Palace, home to the Ottoman Sultans, as the waterfront bends northwards, turning into the Bosphorus. Over the final hilly kilometre runners take a left turn to run inland, ascending through the Palace Gardens, and passing under the shadow of the Byzantine cathedral of Hagia Sophia to finish beside the 300-year-old Blue Mosque – so called because of the 20,000 blue tiles that cover its surface.

The race is in mid-October and a 9.00am start almost guarantees comfortable running conditions. The going is fast, apart from the last kilometre, as the course records of 2:10 and 2:27 would indicate. These were run very recently: the 1985 course record set by Turkey's own Mehmet Terzi took more than 20 years to break. Finally, in 2006, it was improved by a single second.

Istanbul possessed elevated status under the Byzantine Empire, with such grand titles as 'The Great City' and 'City of Emperors', and after taking part in such a prestigious race, runners will feel equally as grand. Those that come to run here say they have not just completed a physical challenge, but absorbed the atmosphere of one of the world's great cities.

Above: The Bosphorus Bridge is 1km (¾ mile long) and the 100,000 competitors who participate in the fun run and marathon.

Tallinn Marathon | Estonia

Estonia's ascendancy to the world marathon stage began in 1989, just two years before that country was declared independent from Russia. After many years of struggling to find numbers and favour with the city authorities, the marathon was re-launched after being cancelled at extremely short notice in 2007. That marathon had an immediate impact and a half marathon and 10km run are now held at the same time.

In Berlin, London and New York, you know what sights lie on the well-trodden marathon route. Head to Tallinn, the capital of Estonia, and you'll be continually surprised by what gems were hidden from view during the Cold War years. Tallinn provides runners with an abundance of history and culture. Locals are proud of their UNESCO World Heritage Site status, as well as their stint as European Capital of Culture in 2011, something that has injected a spirit of optimism for the future of the Baltic. The city and the race are where folk culture meets blue-chip technology. The route begins in the new business district, and moves to take in Tallinn's old quarters, embracing the parks, the old city walls and an old town that is a renowned jewel. There is respite to be had in running along the coastal paths and beside beaches, to the east of the city leading to the Tallinn Marina and beyond.

In September temperatures are usually cool, averaging 8°–15°C (46°–55°F). Such conditions have already secured Tallinn as the biggest marathon field in the Baltic, which, with those in the half marathon, 10km and fun run added in, now totals more than 17,500. Just 1,000 among these run the marathon.

At the last count, 40 different nationalities were registered to run, which given the previous low profile of the country, can be seen as instant success. Visitors have mostly come from Germany, Finland, Britain and Russia but more are flocking from landmark marathon countries as far afield as the US. Estonia has made it state policy to explore the advantages of wireless communication, and the 'green and keen' marathon organisers have followed this up with free rail travel to the race being

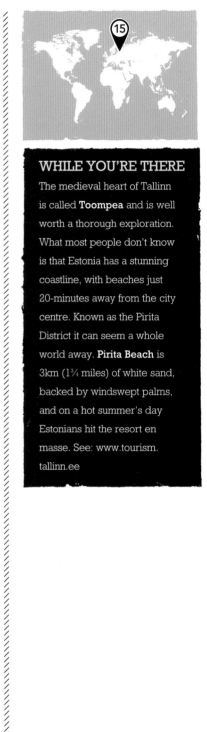

WHILE YOU'RE THERE

The medieval heart of Tallinn is called **Toompea** and is well worth a thorough exploration. What most people don't know is that Estonia has a stunning coastline, with beaches just 20-minutes away from the city centre. Known as the Pirita District it can seem a whole world away. **Pirita Beach** is 3km (1¾ miles) of white sand, backed by windswept palms, and on a hot summer's day Estonians hit the resort en masse. See: www.tourism. tallinn.ee texted to participants' mobile phones. Additionally there is an enthusiasm to embrace the latest marathon technology.

Running here opens your eyes to a thriving community that is now relishing the opportunity to showcase itself. Just one weekend here will give you the chance to sample music shows, exhibitions, and some charming folk traditions – once you're out of your running shorts.

Left: A bird's-eye view of the start of the marathon.

Top: More than 10,000 runners throng the streets on marathon day, including children who have their own race.

Above: The Tallinn Marathon boasts some of the best value entry fees in Europe.

Right: Running the Tallinn Marathon is one of the best ways to see this undiscovered city from a fresh perspective.

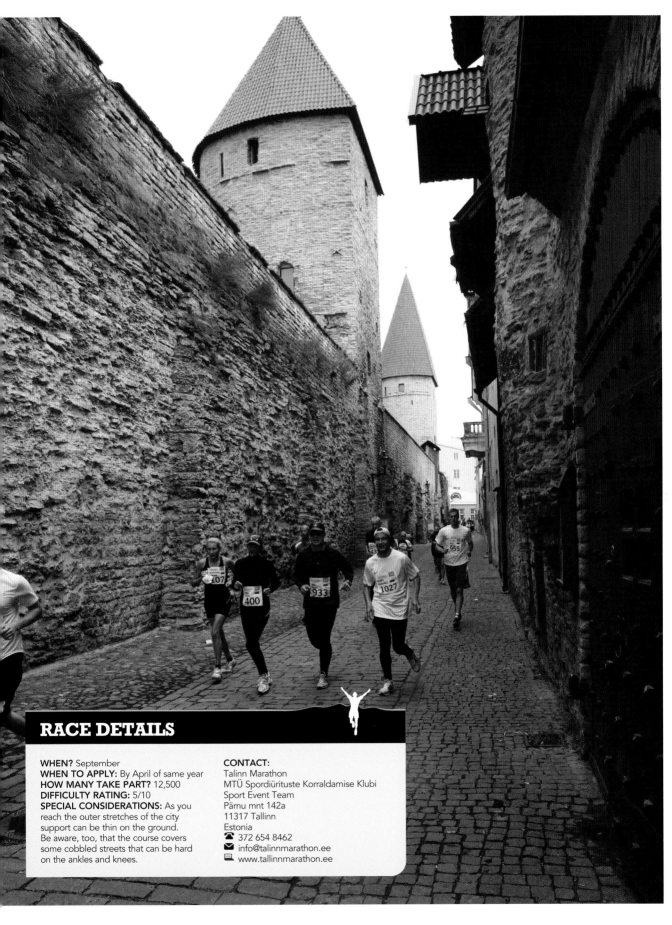

RACE DETAILS

WHEN? September
WHEN TO APPLY: By April of same year
HOW MANY TAKE PART? 12,500
DIFFICULTY RATING: 5/10
SPECIAL CONSIDERATIONS: As you reach the outer stretches of the city support can be thin on the ground. Be aware, too, that the course covers some cobbled streets that can be hard on the ankles and knees.

CONTACT:
Talinn Marathon
MTÜ Spordiürituste Korraldamise Klubi
Sport Event Team
Pärnu mnt 142a
11317 Tallinn
Estonia
☎ 372 654 8462
✉ info@talinnmarathon.ee
🖥 www.tallinnmarathon.ee

Athens Classic
Marathon | Greece

The road from Marathon to Athens is part of mythology. The Marathon legend started here in 490BC, and it was resurrected here under the flag of the Modern Olympic Games in 1896 to become synonymous with any act of sustained endeavour.

The legend has it that a soldier-messenger was sent from Marathon to Athens to announce the victory of the Greeks after they defeated a Persian army of far superior number. A more plausible, and more heroic, version of the story is that the Greek soldiers who had done battle at Marathon, all 11,000 of them, walk-ran from the site of the battle back to Athens to forestall a second landing by the Persian Army.

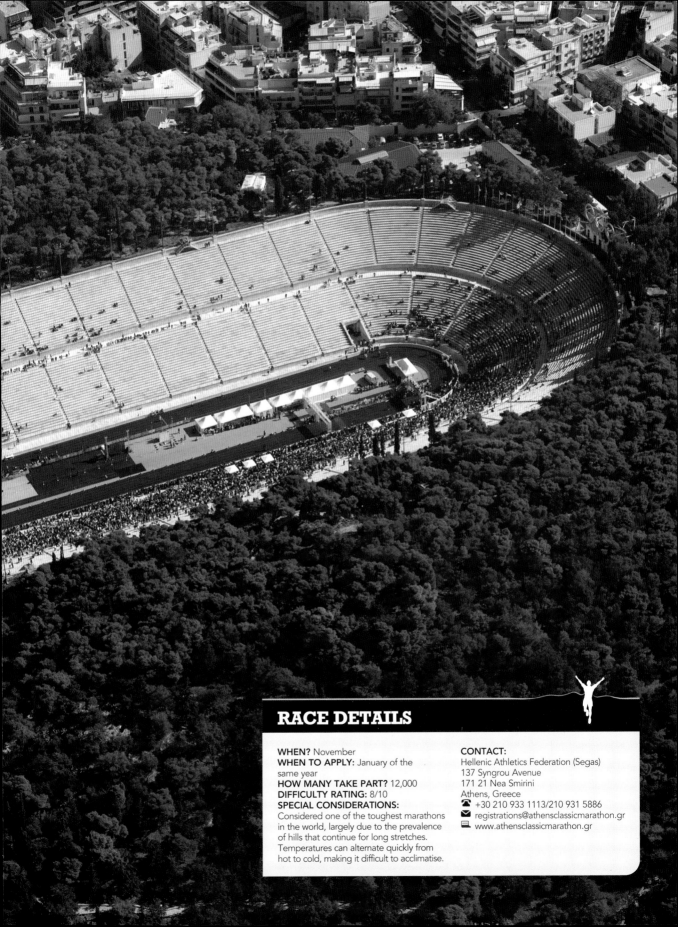

RACE DETAILS

WHEN? November
WHEN TO APPLY: January of the same year
HOW MANY TAKE PART? 12,000
DIFFICULTY RATING: 8/10
SPECIAL CONSIDERATIONS:
Considered one of the toughest marathons in the world, largely due to the prevalence of hills that continue for long stretches. Temperatures can alternate quickly from hot to cold, making it difficult to acclimatise.

CONTACT:
Hellenic Athletics Federation (Segas)
137 Syngrou Avenue
171 21 Nea Smirini
Athens, Greece
☎ +30 210 933 1113/210 931 5886
✉ registrations@athensclassicmarathon.gr
🖥 www.athensclassicmarathon.gr

WHILE YOU'RE THERE

The Greek capital can be
smoggy and claustrophobic,
but its monuments, such as the
Parthenon are a must-see.
Be sure to head out to the coast.
For example, you can take an
overnight ferry to Crete, and
visit the town of **Plakias**, where
beaches are minutes away. Stay
on the mainland and explore
the Attican peninsula. Start off
in Glyfada or Vouliagmeni and
take the sea road to find the
ruins of Sounion, the **Temple of
Poseidon** and the **Sanctuary
of Athena**.

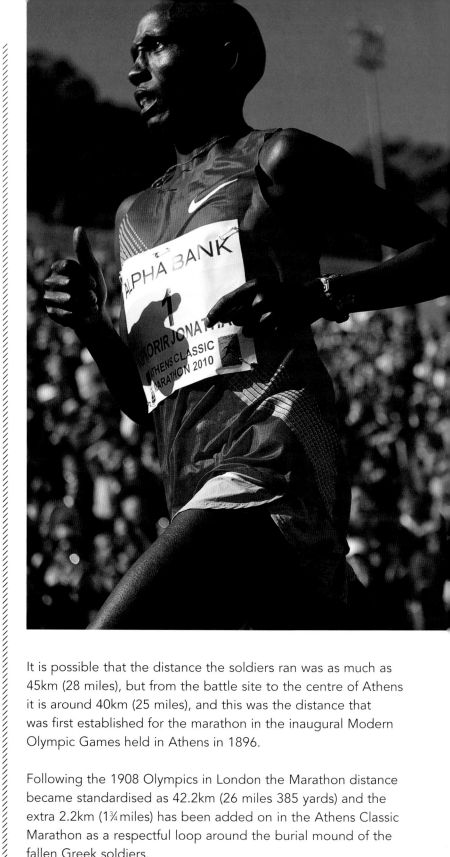

It is possible that the distance the soldiers ran was as much as
45km (28 miles), but from the battle site to the centre of Athens
it is around 40km (25 miles), and this was the distance that
was first established for the marathon in the inaugural Modern
Olympic Games held in Athens in 1896.

Following the 1908 Olympics in London the Marathon distance
became standardised as 42.2km (26 miles 385 yards) and the
extra 2.2km (1¾ miles) has been added on in the Athens Classic
Marathon as a respectful loop around the burial mound of the
fallen Greek soldiers.

The original route was probably over steep terrain, and would have been more like cross-country than road running. Today, there is a modern highway all the way from the marathon start point to the entrance to the stadium built for the 1896 Olympics. The tarmac may be smooth, but the road undulates upward from 11km (6¾ miles) right through to the crest of the hills at 31km (19¼ miles), before dropping down gently towards the centre of Athens. To add yet more drama to the close of this historic race the runners are overlooked by the Parthenon, gleaming white from the top of the nearby Acropolis.

You are likely to see many runners dressed up in the style of the ancient Greek military with helmets and costumes, but nothing can be as arduous as tackling the course while carrying real swords and full body armour as the marathon pioneers may have done. In 2010, the race celebrated the 2,500th anniversary of the Battle of Marathon, and international interest was such that the 12,000 marathon places were snapped up in the space of three weeks. Marathon entries have continued to rise to 16,000 with the more than 20,000 entries in the 10km and 5km races being filled within two days.

The point-to-point route, from the site of the original battlefield in Marathon to the reconstructed stadium in Athens, means that runners are driven out in buses to the start, allowing them a last-minute preview of the route. Due to the event's momentous history the course has been kept as close to the 1896 route as possible, but time has made it more agreeable to modern runners with proper road surfaces, hospitable crowds, and the benefits of comfortable running shoes.

Heading into Athens, there is an instant shift in noise, from the relative tranquillity of the countryside to the traffic horns, buzz, and cheering crowds of the city. As runners enter the final 100m (328ft) in the ancient white marble stadium (which was reconstructed from the remains of the ancient Greek stadium), they can mentally recreate their own imaginings of past glories. Those that take part in this event regard it as a privilege, but will humbly tell you they consider their feat marginal when compared to the soldiers who first embarked on this journey through thick shrubbery and enduring the pain of their battle scars. This is the event where competitors show their respect to those historic running legends.

Previous page: The finale to the marathon is in the spectacular white marble stadium, rebuilt from ancient ruins for the 1896 Olympic Games.

Above: The final 150m (492ft) is run in the marble Panathinaikos Stadium, which was the centrepiece of the first modern Olympic Games, and every step is infused with an emotion appropriate to the historic setting.

Midnight Sun Marathon | Norway

There are few places where running at night can be so exhilarating as at a latitude of 70 degrees north. The Midnight Sun Marathon is an arctic adventure for the running select with 24 hours of daylight providing an almost unworldly experience.

The journey begins in Tromsø, 2,000km (1,240 miles) from the North Pole. Although there is still snow on the hilltops that surround the town, it is a warm and welcoming place. Around 50,000 people live in Tromsø, the unofficial capital of northern Norway, a location that positively brims with culture. This land is defined by the natural majesty of the Northern Lights, Polar Nights and the Midnight Sun.

In summer, the sun doesn't set for two months. The distinctive atmosphere that this creates throughout the night provides a thrilling warm-up to the world's northernmost continental marathon. The climate is moderate enough, offering mild conditions on race day – summer weather ranges from 5–28°C (41–82°F). Runners from more than 60 nations take part, coming from the UK, USA, Germany, Sweden, Italy, Brazil and Australia. Alongside the marathon, there is a half marathon, a 10km race and a mini-marathon, as well as a children's race.

The course begins with a loop into the city centre before runners pass Fridtjof Nansen Square – named after the pioneering polar explorer – and climb up over the 1,026m (3,360ft)-long Tromsø Bridge, which rises to 44m (144ft) above sea level. Reaching the mainland, runners pass the Arctic Cathedral and head down the coast road to a turning point after about 10km. Returning back over the bridge, the half marathoners peel off to the finish, but marathon runners go on through the centre of the city and around the southern part of the island before heading north into the midnight sun. After another turnaround, the course returns to finish in the city centre, where the town spills out onto the streets to cheer in the finishers with an uplifting fervour.

WHILE YOU'RE THERE

The locals celebrate hard at the end of a marathon. But be sure to reserve energy for some daytime exploration, as the region offers some of the most beautiful natural majesty in the world. This reveals itself in the **weather-beaten islands** of the Arctic Ocean, **blue fjords**, **glaciers** and the towering peaks of the 1,800m (5,900ft)-high **Lyngen Alps**. The tepid waters of the Gulf Stream ensure a mild climate at high latitude, offering maximum chance of experiencing the colourful rays of the **Northern Lights**, as well as the golden warmth of the midnight sun. See: www.visitnorway.com

The inhabitants of Tromsø regard the Midnight Sun Marathon as one of the big spectacles that brings the world to its doorstep. Other popular attractions in the city are the Arctic Cathedral, the Tromsø Museum, the Polar Museum, and a cable car which runs up a nearby hilltop. Despite its location in the far north of Norway, Tromsø has the cosmopolitan feel of a larger city, with inhabitants from 130 different countries, a vibrant nightlife, and charming coffee shops, bars and restaurants. Just a short distance outside the city lies one of Norway's most photogenic regions with fjords and mountains aplenty, crowned by snow even in midsummer.

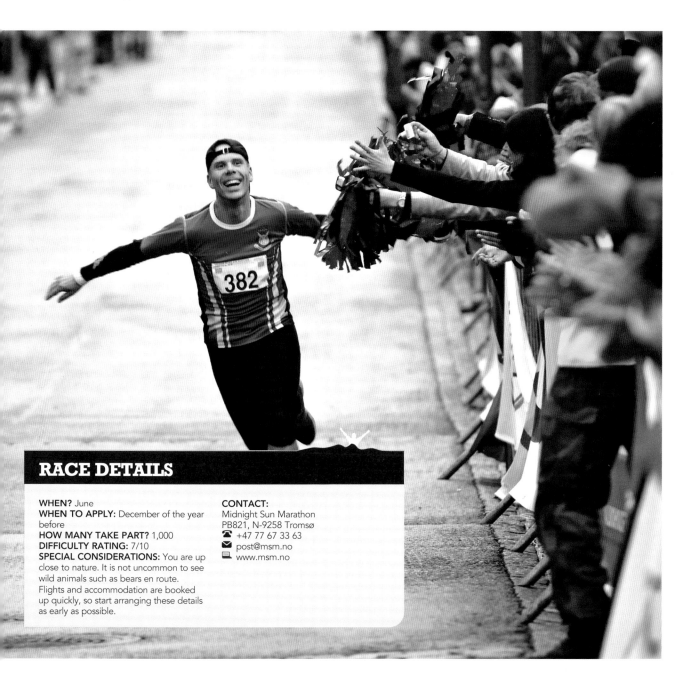

Below: The Midnight Sun Marathon begins at 8.30pm in the evening and has enthusiastic crowd support.

RACE DETAILS

WHEN? June
WHEN TO APPLY: December of the year before
HOW MANY TAKE PART? 1,000
DIFFICULTY RATING: 7/10
SPECIAL CONSIDERATIONS: You are up close to nature. It is not uncommon to see wild animals such as bears en route. Flights and accommodation are booked up quickly, so start arranging these details as early as possible.

CONTACT:
Midnight Sun Marathon
PB821, N-9258 Tromsø
☎ +47 77 67 33 63
✉ post@msm.no
🖥 www.msm.no

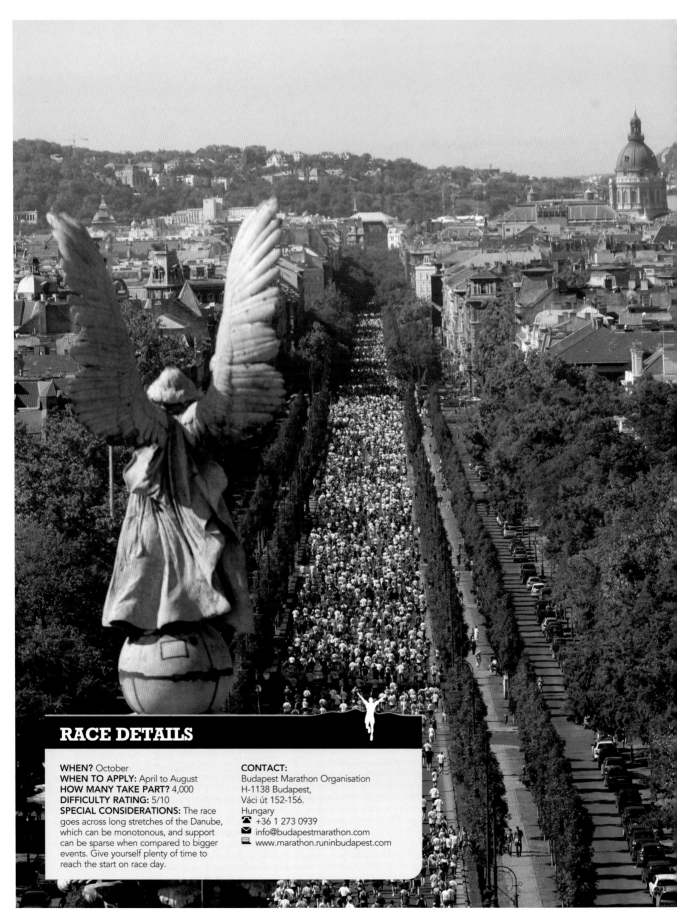

RACE DETAILS

WHEN? October
WHEN TO APPLY: April to August
HOW MANY TAKE PART? 4,000
DIFFICULTY RATING: 5/10
SPECIAL CONSIDERATIONS: The race
goes across long stretches of the Danube,
which can be monotonous, and support
can be sparse when compared to bigger
events. Give yourself plenty of time to
reach the start on race day.

CONTACT:
Budapest Marathon Organisation
H-1138 Budapest,
Váci út 152-156.
Hungary
☎ +36 1 273 0939
✉ info@budapestmarathon.com
🖳 www.marathon.runinbudapest.com

Budapest Marathon | Hungary

Hungary's capital offers a culture-rich experience for the runner and the traveller alike. It is a city of architectural splendour which spreads along the broad sweep of the Danube River, and its marathon takes you on a tour through the very best parts.

Budapest was once two separate cities but the town of Buda, nestling among the hills of the Danube's west bank, was united with Pest, on the flat eastern bank, in 1873.

For much of its length, the course runs along the lower embankments of the river, affording a panorama of the Buda Hills from the Pest side and views of the magnificent Neo-Gothic dome Parliament House from the Buda side, as well as crossing two, and sometimes three, of the famous Danube bridges.

The race starts in the iconic statue-lined Hosök Tere, or Heroes' Square and loops back to finish nearby after its grand tour of the Hungarian capital. The heroes referred to are not of the Soviet era (although a giant statue of Stalin which was once sited close to the present finish line was toppled from its plinth in the 1956 Hungarian Uprising). Heroes' Square was built in 1896 to mark the millennium of the founding of the Hungarian state and the statuary lining the monument's porticoes are primarily those of previous kings. Runners exit the impressive, open square along the tree-lined Andrássy út, a UNESCO World Heritage site, passing Béla Bartók Memorial Museum and the majestic Hungarian State Opera House.

Where you go from here depends on which year you run the race. There has been so much renovation in Budapest over the last few years that the course has to be changed every year to navigate a way through the works. The most recent edition involved a loop through Margaret Island to the north before returning to the city centre and crossing the Danube by means of the iconic Chain Bridge, the first permanent link between the two sides of the river, originally built in 1849. Once on the other side runners loop south around Castle Hill before cutting

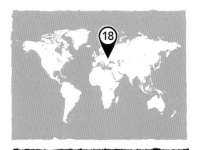

WHILE YOU'RE THERE

Buda is the older part of the city and good for exploration, while Pest has the edge for eating. By daytime head to the **Neo-Gothic Parliament** buildings, with a design based on the Houses of Parliament in London. It is the country's largest and most impressive building. By night, catch a show at **The Hungarian State Opera**, a bargain by many other capital city prices. Even more impressive than any show is the building, with marble hallways, crystal chandeliers and acres of gilt, creating a Belle Époque fantasy land. See: www. visitbudapest.travel

Left: Looking south down Andrássy út as runners leave Heroes Square at the start of the race.

through the tunnel under it and back to the Embankment. Runners can't resist testing the echo in the tunnel.

The route continues under the Chain Bridge and past the 'Rudas' thermal baths dating from the Ottoman occupation 400 years ago. After the next turnaround point runners loop back past the Technical University to the Art Deco Gellert Hotel from where they cross the Liberty Bridge. On the Pest side there is one more turnaround point before they head north along the lower embankment to bypass the city centre and the impressive Neo-Gothic domed Parliament building before completing the Margaret Island loop in reverse.

Finally, turning away from the river in front of the Parliament, the last few kilometres confront you with the biggest rise on this mainly flat course – a flyover taking runners over the inner ring road, a route necessary to avoid closing Europe's busiest tram system.

Left: The Chain Bridge is the first that runners cross in the Budapest Marathon.

Above: Much of the on-course support has to come from fellow runners still approaching the turns after you have made yours, as the lower embankments leave little room for bystanders.

Like the other capital of the Habsburg 'dual-monarchy' Empire, Vienna, Budapest makes music a theme of the marathon, with classical concerts performing in full swing as the race comes to an end. Tired runners can flock to Budapest's many spas, which are a welcome delight to ease the pains of the runners. Choose the 19th-century Szechenyi Bath and Spa conveniently close to the finish line in the City Park, or return to the Rudas Thermal Baths in Buda, dating from the 16th and 17th centuries, and redolent with atmosphere. The evocative surroundings and the promise of a thermal bath at the end of the race make the Budapest Marathon an inviting prospect.

Cape Town Marathon and Two Oceans Marathon | South Africa

Table Mountain in Cape Town provides a stunningly beautiful backdrop, and there are several races organised to take advantage of it. The Cape Town Marathon is run in September, and the more high profile Two Oceans Marathon – which is a 56km (35 miles) ultra-distance race – is held on Easter Saturday each year, along with a highly popular half marathon.

Like races all over South Africa, the Cape Town Marathon starts at 6.30am to take advantage of the cooler conditions. Water stations are placed regularly throughout the course to ensure runners keep well hydrated. The fast, flat route of the marathon starts in Cape Town's city centre and takes runners out to Rondebosch before looping back to the City and the Victoria & Alfred Waterfront, Sea Point and the Green Point Common.

Many runners turn out for the Cape Town Marathon to chase times that will qualify them to run in one of South Africa's racing spectacles, such as the Comrades Marathon in Durban (89km/55 miles), or more locally, the Two Oceans Marathon.

WHILE YOU'RE THERE

The **Victoria & Alfred Waterfront** offers the sight of one of the most beautiful natural harbours in the world. Take advantage of the hotels – the **Table Bay Hotel** offers great views across the ocean to **Robben Island**, and the best afternoon teas in the country, with many travelling from further afield to sample the delicacies on offer (www.hoteltablebay.co.za). Nearby is the **Cape Grace**, best visited in the evening for Africa's finest collection of whisky.

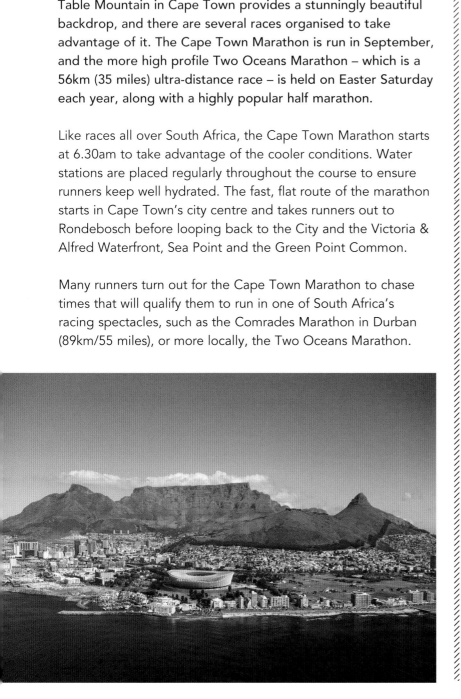

Left: A flat, fast course amid spectacular scenery of mountains and sea make this an appealing marathon.

Right: The Two Oceans Marathon and its associated trail run (pictured) lives up to its reputation as a tough endurance run.

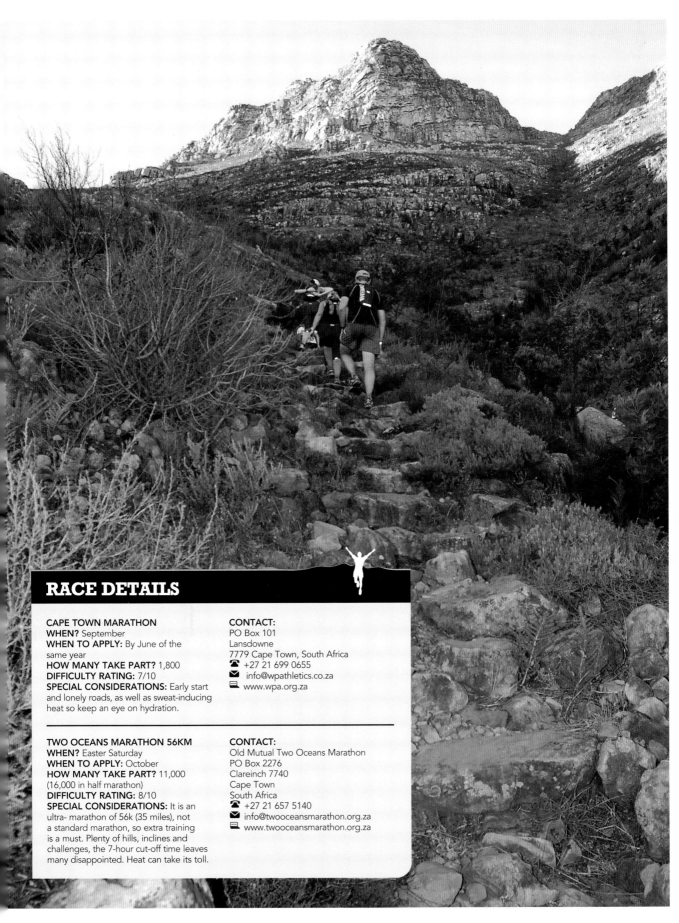

RACE DETAILS

CAPE TOWN MARATHON
WHEN? September
WHEN TO APPLY: By June of the same year
HOW MANY TAKE PART? 1,800
DIFFICULTY RATING: 7/10
SPECIAL CONSIDERATIONS: Early start and lonely roads, as well as sweat-inducing heat so keep an eye on hydration.

CONTACT:
PO Box 101
Lansdowne
7779 Cape Town, South Africa
☎ +27 21 699 0655
✉ info@wpathletics.co.za
🖳 www.wpa.org.za

TWO OCEANS MARATHON 56KM
WHEN? Easter Saturday
WHEN TO APPLY: October
HOW MANY TAKE PART? 11,000
(16,000 in half marathon)
DIFFICULTY RATING: 8/10
SPECIAL CONSIDERATIONS: It is an ultra- marathon of 56k (35 miles), not a standard marathon, so extra training is a must. Plenty of hills, inclines and challenges, the 7-hour cut-off time leaves many disappointed. Heat can take its toll.

CONTACT:
Old Mutual Two Oceans Marathon
PO Box 2276
Clareinch 7740
Cape Town
South Africa
☎ +27 21 657 5140
✉ info@twooceansmarathon.org.za
🖳 www.twooceansmarathon.org.za

Two Oceans adds another third to the standard marathon distance, although not as long as many races in South Africa's running calendar, which is dominated by ultra-distance races. However, in contrast to the Cape Town Marathon the course is far from 'flat and fast', although runners may be encouraged by the relative flatness of the first half before they start the climb up to Chapman's Peak (180m/590ft). After dropping down from there to Hout Bay the course climbs again to the highest point at Constantia Nek (215m/705ft) and then follows an undulating route to the finish at the University of Cape Town. To qualify, runners must have completed a marathon in under five hours.

Left: There is much truth in the organisers' claim that the Two Ocean Marathon is 'the world's most beautiful marathon', despite the fact that it is not technically a marathon.

Above: Wild, windy weather can make conditions difficult for even the most experienced runners.

The Two Oceans route takes in the gardens of Kirstenbosch and the vast sweep of coastline from Fish Hoek, cutting through the Cape Town peninsula to Chapman's Peak. In doing so, it lives up to its name and takes in the coastlines of the Atlantic and Indian Oceans in one glorious sweep.

The tipping point comes during the mountain climb known as the 'Suikerbossie Pass'. When all reserves are spent, the reward is the sight of the Atlantic Ocean glistening in the distance, and the memory of it will stay with you for years.

RACE DETAILS

WHEN? End of May/Start of June
WHEN TO APPLY: January of the same year
HOW MANY TAKE PART? 21,000
DIFFICULTY RATING: 7/10
SPECIAL CONSIDERATIONS: Unlike many marathons, this one starts in the afternoon, so if the weather is a scorching, conditions can become uncomfortable.

CONTACT:
Stockholm Marathon
15124, SE-16715 Bromma
Sweden
☎ +46 8 545 664 40
✉ info@stockholmmarathon.se
🖥 www.stockholmmarathon.se

Stockholm Marathon
Sweden

The story of Stockholm's marathon shows that with grit and determination almost anyone can set up a marathon. Anders Olsson founded the Stockholm Marathon to boost the profile of distance running in Scandinavia. He remembers, 'On my long journey home on the subway one November day in 1978, I was dazzled by an article in *Sports Illustrated* magazine. It was about the New York City Marathon, with 21,000 runners pacing the streets across the Big Apple. I was really inspired. What a contrast to the lukewarm and isolated Swedish running scene. This was a race to attend. But then I had second thoughts. Why should you have to go to New York? Couldn't we replicate the success story in Stockholm?'.

20

WHILE YOU'RE THERE

Sweden's capital is home to a vast, fan-shaped maritime world of more than 24,000 islets. In summer, the **Archipelago** is a paradise for sailors and boaters and also accessible to visitors travelling by public transport. An hour by bus, local train or car will take you to various island communities.

The best option, however, is to depart from central Stockholm on one of the **classic white ferries**, many of which date from the 19th and early 20th centuries. Once there you can explore the sheer natural beauty of the islands – most are well-served with **hotels**, **inns**, **campsites** and **restaurants**. See: www.visitsweden.com

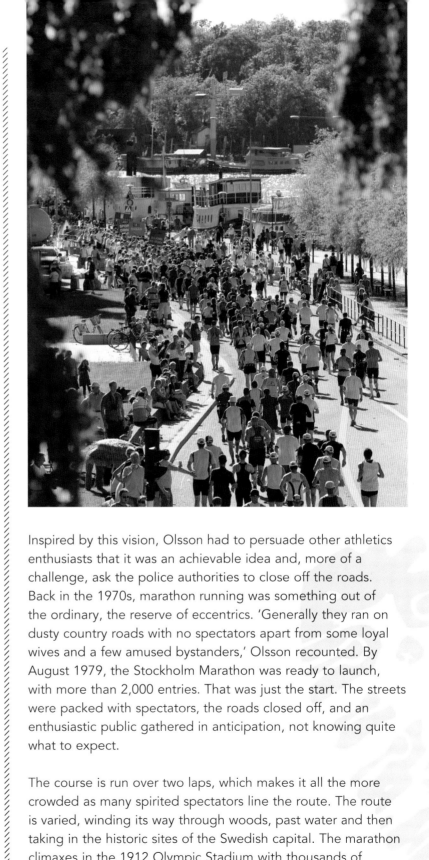

Inspired by this vision, Olsson had to persuade other athletics enthusiasts that it was an achievable idea and, more of a challenge, ask the police authorities to close off the roads. Back in the 1970s, marathon running was something out of the ordinary, the reserve of eccentrics. 'Generally they ran on dusty country roads with no spectators apart from some loyal wives and a few amused bystanders,' Olsson recounted. By August 1979, the Stockholm Marathon was ready to launch, with more than 2,000 entries. That was just the start. The streets were packed with spectators, the roads closed off, and an enthusiastic public gathered in anticipation, not knowing quite what to expect.

The course is run over two laps, which makes it all the more crowded as many spirited spectators line the route. The route is varied, winding its way through woods, past water and then taking in the historic sites of the Swedish capital. The marathon climaxes in the 1912 Olympic Stadium with thousands of

Previous page: Runners pass along the waterside around the old town in Stockholm.

Left: The course takes in two laps around the medieval city, the waterways and forest.

Above: The run begins outside the 1912 Olympic stadium and finishes on a track inside, to much enthusiastic crowd support.

fans waiting to cheer on those finishing. The stadium has been the venue for 83 world records and with 8,500 international runners from more than 81 countries, this marathon is a multicultural festival.

Part of the draw is Stockholm, one of the world's most beautiful capitals. Built on 14 islands around its medieval city centre, it is superbly positioned, with stunning scenic views in every direction. The archipelago of 24,000 islets is waiting to be explored just outside the city. Stockholm is a city of contrasts: water and islands, history and innovation, small town and big city, long light summer nights and short winter days. The course embraces the best of the capital, heading into the woods of the Royal Djurgården Park and through the streets of the city centre, passing buildings such as the Royal Palace, the City Hall, the Royal Opera and the Houses of Parliament. Crossing the high, arching Västerbron Bridge at the western end of the course, runners are rewarded with a fantastic view over the city.

Vienna City Marathon | Austria

The race slogan of the Vienna City Marathon is 'Run Vienna, Enjoy Classics' and this spirit is borne out in a number of ways, from runners in Amadeus wigs to mini classical concerts along the route. This is a race run against a backdrop of classical Hapsburg architecture and an accompaniment of classical music from great composers – after all, this was Mozart's city.

Vienna has inspired musicians with its rich classical past. Its effect on runners is little different. The unexpected melody of a string quartet will lift the spirit when their energy levels flag. To onlookers, it is a race set to an operatic soundtrack. In fact, you may often be buoyed along the route by the music of composers such as Mozart and Strauss. In previous years the much-revered Sir Simon Rattle has conducted special concerts for the race.

Runners come from more than 100 countries to make up a total field of 30,000. The course includes many long, flat stretches of road and expanses of greenery. The scenic tour of the city is enough to keep morale up. This is a good venue for first-timers.

WHILE YOU'RE THERE

Be sure to head to the **Hofburg Castle**, once the heart of the Austro-Hungarian Empire, and now the heart of Vienna – its parks, churches and museums all surround it. Meander through the lanes and the world-famous coffee houses, the rendez-vous of many an intellectual. If you want to go further afield, head to **Belvedere Palace** in the 3rd District, the hub of Vienna's classical art collection, including Gustav Klimt's *The Kiss*. Equally impressive is the **Schönbrunn Palace**. It was built to rival France's Versailles in Baroque beauty, but the House of Habsburg lacked the funds to outdo its French rival. See: www.austria.info

Left: Other runs take place at the same time as the marathon in this attractive and scenic city.

Right: The Vienna City Marathon attracts many elite athletes. This photo shows the old finish line, which has now been superseded.

RACE DETAILS

WHEN? April
WHEN TO APPLY: By November of the year before
HOW MANY TAKE PART? 30,000
DIFFICULTY RATING: 5/10
SPECIAL CONSIDERATIONS: Cut-off time here is 6 hours, but the clearing up operation can happen before that.

CONTACT:
Enterprise Sport Promotion GmbH
Gußhausstruße 21/19
1040 Vienna, Austria
☎ +43 1 606 421 95 10
✉ office@vienna-marathon.com
🖥 www.vienna-marathon.com

In fact, one edition of the race limited the elite field to 'debutantes only'.

The race begins with a long straight crossing of the Donaukanal (Danube canal), passing beside the city's UN Building and finishes by turning off the inner ring road under an archway. Abruptly you find yourself at the Heldenplatz (or Heroes' Square), right in front of the Imperial Palace. Along the route you cross the Danube, past the iconic Ferris Wheel in Wiener Prater (Prater Park) and run in front of the Schönbrunn Palace. The Opera House is perhaps the classical building that has made the city so recognisable around the world, and it is also included in the runners' tour offered by the marathon.

Above: Athletes from more than 100 countries take part in this popular event.

Right: The Vienna City Marathon was among the first to offer technical assistance to its runners and their supporters. It pioneered a text messaging service that alerted participants to split times recorded every 5km (3 miles) allowing any runner's progress to be tracked and their finishing time anticipated.

The crowds are vocal and their support is always welcome. Even as a stranger you will still feel as if your own relatives are urging you on toward the finishing line. The support is not just confined to the race. Race organisers have created a network to encourage runners to come to Vienna from further afield. The VCM Friendship Runners are local volunteers who have run the race before and can assist newcomers by answering questions and exchanging information in their own language through the website: www.vienna-marathon.com.

The handling of this event is superbly organised, and not without elements of fun. Each year the marathon is themed around a key event. In 2010 this included celebrating the 2,500 year anniversary of the Battle of Marathon in Greece.

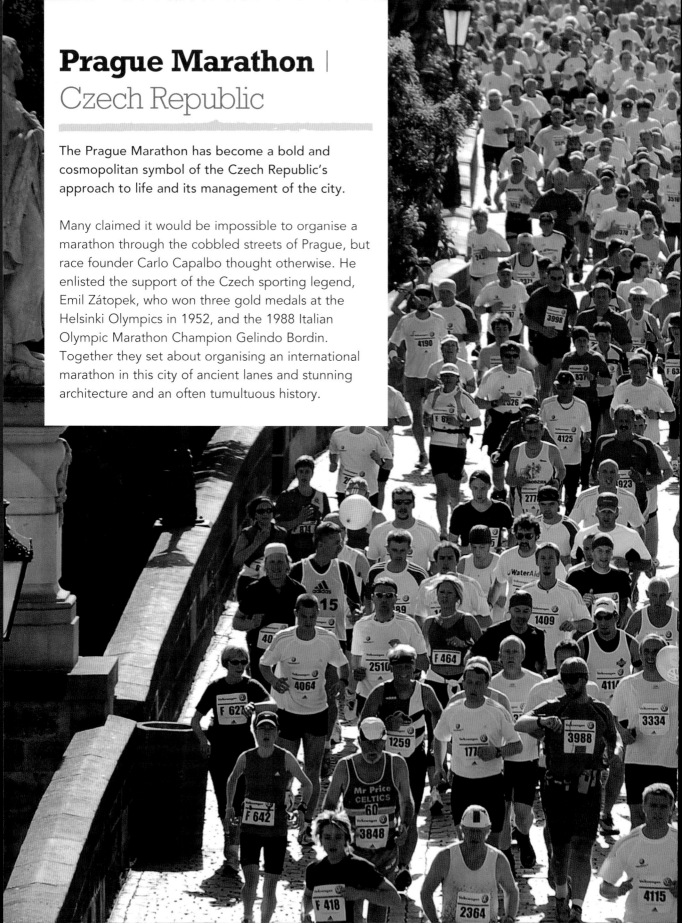

Prague Marathon | Czech Republic

The Prague Marathon has become a bold and cosmopolitan symbol of the Czech Republic's approach to life and its management of the city.

Many claimed it would be impossible to organise a marathon through the cobbled streets of Prague, but race founder Carlo Capalbo thought otherwise. He enlisted the support of the Czech sporting legend, Emil Zátopek, who won three gold medals at the Helsinki Olympics in 1952, and the 1988 Italian Olympic Marathon Champion Gelindo Bordin. Together they set about organising an international marathon in this city of ancient lanes and stunning architecture and an often tumultuous history.

RACE DETAILS

WHEN? May
WHEN TO APPLY: By January
HOW MANY TAKE PART? 11,000
DIFFICULTY RATING: 6/10
SPECIAL CONSIDERATIONS: Recent participants have reported logistical problems at the start, and the narrow cobblestone streets can be difficult for those with ankle or knee problems.

CONTACT:
Prague International Marathon, spol.s.r.o.
Františka Křižka 11
170 00 Praha 7
Czech Republic
☎ +420 224 91 92 09
✉ info@runczech.com
🖳 www.runczech.com

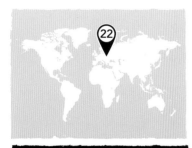

WHILE YOU'RE THERE

Prague is one of the most well-preserved cities in Europe, and a meander through the **old city** reveals fascinating sites. An essential is a visit to the **Charles Bridge**, as much a work of art as a feat of engineering. Spend an afternoon wondering across and up to the medieval **Prague Castle**, marvelling at the architecture, including Gothic, Renaissance and Art Nouveau.

Since its foundation in 1995, when just 958 runners lined up at the start of the race, the Prague Marathon has grown into one of the most magical and exciting international marathons.

Prague is a city that is animated by the arts. Marathon Music Festival is held alongside the race and hosts professional and amateur bands all along the course, setting the beat for runners' steps. The music attracts crowds on to the streets, providing support for the runners and creating an unmistakable atmosphere. The Prague race begins each year with a rendition of the beloved Czech theme 'Vltava', from Bedrich Smetana's composition, 'Ma Vlast' (My Country), a piece of music that is reminiscent of the sound of a flowing river. As the music plays, the composition seems to embrace the river of runners flooding over the start line at the Old Town Square. From the starting gun, they begin their swift flow through the streets and alongside the Vltava River.

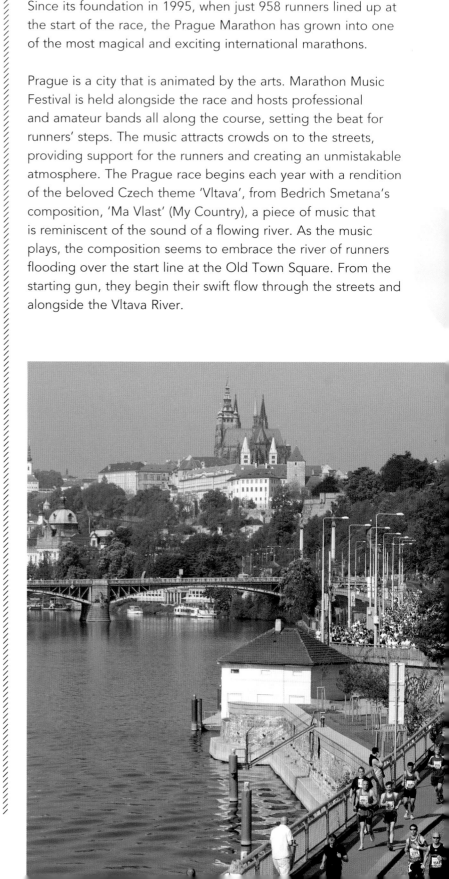

Reaching the river after a few hundred metres, runners benefit from views of Prague Castle, the ancient seat of Czech kings and the current seat of the Czech President, on the other side. Runners pass the Czech Parliament, the Rudolfinum Concert Hall and the Municipal Hall where every year, following the marathon, the Prague Spring Music Festival begins. Still only in the second kilometre the course then passes through the National Library Quarter, National Theatre and Prague Karolinum, the seat of the Charles University, the oldest university in Central Europe.

The course then crosses back over the river by the famous Charles Bridge, which forms the logo of the Prague Marathon. Treading in the footsteps of more recent history, runners pass down the National Avenue where the former Czechoslovakia's post-communist era began in the student-led Velvet Revolution on 17 November 1989. The final 400m (¼ mile) follows the first part of the course in reverse.

Below: The Prague waterfront is an attractive route for runners.

Below right: The old city monuments are never far away in this marathon.

Bottom right: Paris (Parizska) street is Prague's most famous shopping street, which is always packed with thousands of spectators cheering the runners on to the finishing line.

Berlin Marathon | Germany

The BMW Berlin Marathon is a race where German reserve is broken and emotions run high. It is known as the course where the most world records have been set and where tears are often shed at the Brandenburg Gate finishing line.

Every aspect of the environment is conducive to running. There is the flat and even course, the mild autumn weather, and the atmosphere of the crowd that ripples like an electric current to spur even the most exhausted runners home. Competition is high for amateurs and elite participants alike – elite runners petition for a place in Berlin because they know the course is so favourable for fast times. The last seven men's world records in the marathon have been set in Berlin.

More than 40,000 participants take part in the race and spectators flock to the streets, alongside more than 70 live bands. In some spots, the race becomes a carnival – especially at 'Wilde Eber', around 27km (16¾ miles) into the race, where a group of cheerleaders raise the tempo as the course crests and then gently descends towards the Kurfürstendamm.

The first Berlin Marathon was staged in the Grunewald forest in 1974 in the southwest of the city. It came out of the woods and on to the streets of West Berlin in 1981 but it was only in 1990, after the fall of the Berlin Wall, that the marathon burst through the Brandenburg Gate and embraced the old East Berlin. This was a landmark marathon event that ranks alongside the great centennial 1996 Boston Marathon, or the cathartic 2001 New York City race, just weeks following the 9/11 attacks.

The course now weaves its way past Berlin's historic landmarks, such as the Reichstag, Alexanderplatz, Kufurstendamm, Potsdamer Platz and the Gendarmenmarkt before climaxing at 41km (26 miles) where you pass under the Brandenburg Gate with just 350m (¼ mile) to run to the finish line. Berlin's architecture provides an animated tour of its history, and running a marathon through it is the best possible way to experience the sights in a few hours.

WHILE YOU'RE THERE

The **Reichstag** offers great views over the city from its rooftop dome, while nearby, Berlin's 'museum island' is packed with galleries. Both are within walking distance from the **Brandenburg Gate**.
Berlin is packed with more than 200 clubs, many in revamped theatres such as Schaubühne and Roter Salon. Concerts at the **Berliner Philharmoniker** offer a chance to enjoy some of the best classical music in Europe. See: www.visitberlin.de/en

Right: The route of the Berlin Marathon changed in 1990, just three days before German reunification to run through the Brandenburg Gate and unite both halves of this formerly divided city.

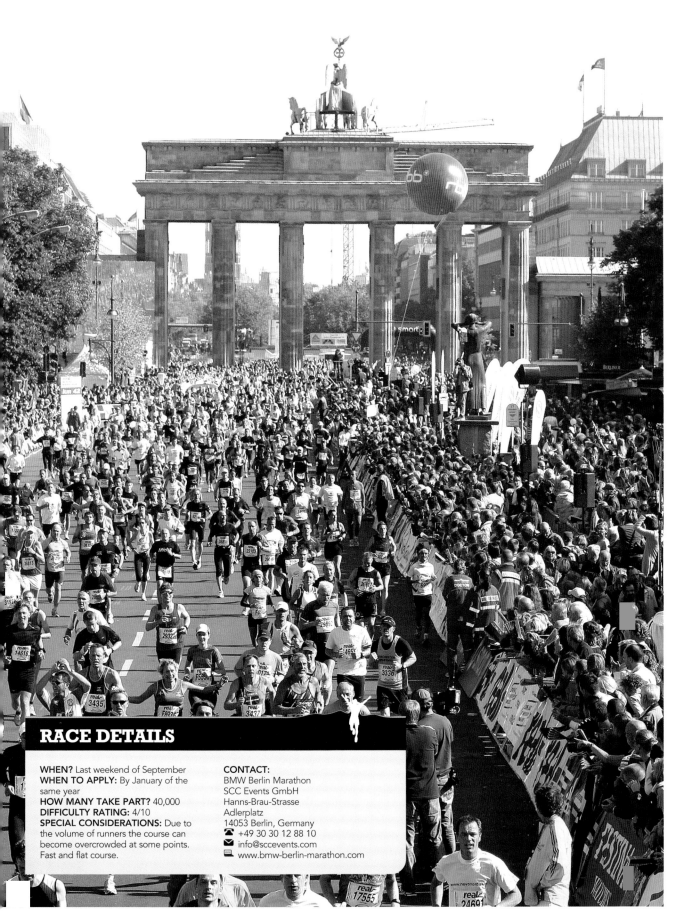

RACE DETAILS

WHEN? Last weekend of September
WHEN TO APPLY: By January of the same year
HOW MANY TAKE PART? 40,000
DIFFICULTY RATING: 4/10
SPECIAL CONSIDERATIONS: Due to the volume of runners the course can become overcrowded at some points. Fast and flat course.

CONTACT:
BMW Berlin Marathon
SCC Events GmbH
Hanns-Brau-Strasse
Adlerplatz
14053 Berlin, Germany
☎ +49 30 30 12 88 10
✉ info@sccevents.com
🖥 www.bmw-berlin-marathon.com

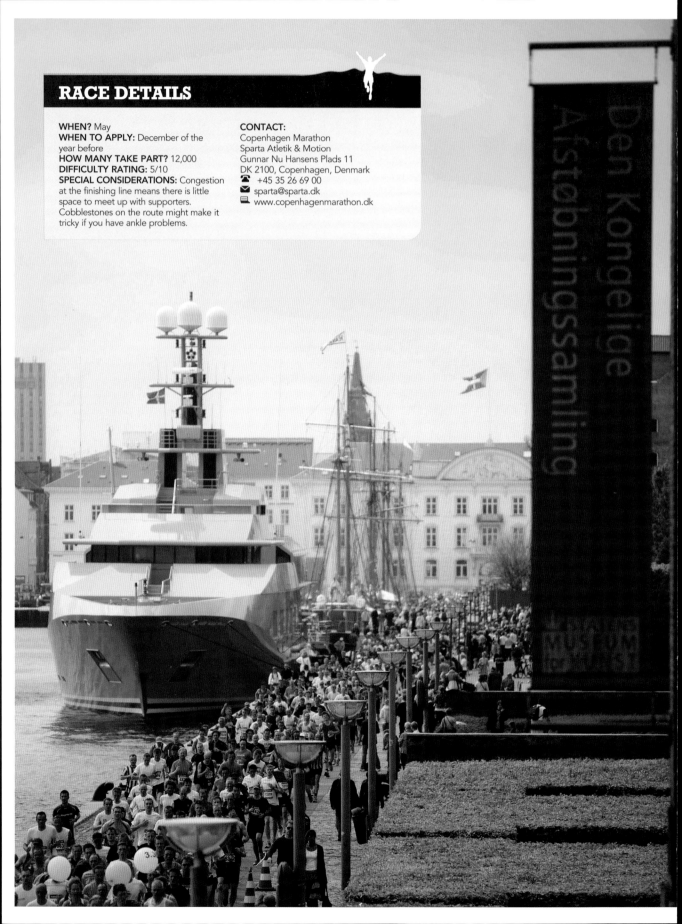

RACE DETAILS

WHEN? May
WHEN TO APPLY: December of the year before
HOW MANY TAKE PART? 12,000
DIFFICULTY RATING: 5/10
SPECIAL CONSIDERATIONS: Congestion at the finishing line means there is little space to meet up with supporters. Cobblestones on the route might make it tricky if you have ankle problems.

CONTACT:
Copenhagen Marathon
Sparta Atletik & Motion
Gunnar Nu Hansens Plads 11
DK 2100, Copenhagen, Denmark
☎ +45 35 26 69 00
✉ sparta@sparta.dk
🖵 www.copenhagenmarathon.dk

Copenhagen Marathon | Denmark

Some races are about the scenery, some are about the spirit of the event, but Copenhagen is all about the running. Competition is keen and even the most amateur enthusiasts are rivals.

This dedication to running is defined in the unofficial slogan of the Copenhagen Marathon 'It's all about the race'. Even so, you'll still be taken on a tour around the iconic landmarks of the Danish capital. There is the Little Mermaid statue down by the harbour, the grand Parliament Building, and all around is the fresh, reviving air of the lakes, parks and green spaces. The run takes in all facets of this city from family-friendly districts, to the finishing line at Langebro with views over the waterfront. Runners are well serviced en route, with hydration stations every 4.5km (2¾ miles) offering energy drinks, toilets, showers and tubs of petroleum jelly to relieve the inevitable chafing sores.

Copenhagen welcomes new runners and has set up pace-setting groups to assist first-timers. A leading athletics group, the Sparta Club, groups runners according to their expected finishing time, helping them to ease through the course at a rhythm which will allow them to reach the finish within their target time. The slowest groups finish in 5 hours, making room for walking breaks, toilet stops, and throwing in heavy doses of morale-boosting songs and inspiration. If you find yourself flagging in one group you can find another slower group, all clearly identifiable by pace runners carrying balloons.

Copenhagen's tradition of communal space allows runners coming here to feel part of one big family. Much of the route is through family districts where spectators tuck into bacon sandwiches in between rousing cheers. There is a mini-marathon of 1km (¾ mile) for children as part of the race's Sports Expo. The Expo is a meeting place full of energy and pre-race adrenaline where you can buy running gear or get a warm-up massage.

Left: In Copenhagen every detail has been addressed, so you can concentrate on the one big reason for coming – the race.

WHILE YOU'RE THERE

Copenhagen has an excellent public transport system including its world-famous city bikes used by visitors and locals alike. The city of Copenhagen keeps expanding its network of **bicycle lanes** and routes and you are likely to get around town faster by bike than by any other means.

The **harbour cruise** is a great introduction to the beauty of the **medieval city**, including the **17th-century stock exchange** and **Nybrogade**.

Venice Marathon | Italy

The question for the Venice Marathon organisation team was how to stage a marathon within a place famous for the lack of any significant land. The answer was to utilise the many bridges that span the floating city of Venice. Bridges are so crucial to this race that one is specially created for the event, a 170m (557ft) floating construction that straddles the Grand Canal. The pontoon gives runners a 360-degree view of central Venice and its most famous square, St Mark's. Such views are not available to anyone but the marathon runners, not even the well-heeled tourists who pay five-figure sums for lavish hotel suites can secure such a fine view. The prominence of the bridges is highlighted by the fact that during the final 3km (1¾ miles) of the marathon there are 13 bridges to cross.

The start of the marathon is on the mainland in front of the 18th-century Villa Pisani in a village called Stra that was originally built for Italian nobility. The route heads through the countryside toward the industrial town of Mestre, reached after 25km (15½ miles). This is a part of the course that you may never see in the photographs. Beyond lies the large green space of San Giuliano Park, in which runners complete a 2km (1¼ miles) section and ready themselves for the 5km (3 mile) crossing of Ponta della Liberta, or Liberty Bridge, the causeway leading to Venice itself. It is here that the frontrunners make their bid to win, but those setting their own pace may find that appreciating the view of the Venetian skyline, looming ever closer, slows their progress a little. Once you're in the town, the view changes to a series of more urban close-ups, apart from the amazing views of supporters from the pontoon bridge.

Negotiating the bridges demands due care and attention. Past the finish line, the water becomes something to be sought out rather than avoided as runners soak their tired legs in the lagoon and find food, drink, massages and a change of clothes arriving by water taxi. But running through Venice at marathon-time helps you glimpse a city that is unknown to other visitors, sweeping in and out of tight alleyways, canalside paths, and gaping squares. The event's officially adopted charity, Water Aid, fits in neatly with its exhortation to 'Run for Water, Run for Life'.

WHILE YOU'RE THERE

Venetians love their football as you would expect of any Italian city. Here if you wish to spectate, you arrive at the stadium in the historic centre by water. After the match there is a great pub-crawl along **Via Garibaldi**, where drink prices beat the average tourist traps. Alternatively grab a seat in one of the local pubs screening Italian Serie A matches. **The Rialto Market,** with its noisy fishmongers and colourful vegetable stalls, is surrounded by many bars and this is where most of Venice converges for weekend feasts.

Right: If you want to take part, make sure you book early – entries are limited to 6,000 each year to prevent undue wear and tear on this World Heritage Site.

RACE DETAILS

WHEN? October
WHEN TO APPLY: January to March
HOW MANY TAKE PART? 6,000
DIFFICULTY RATING: 5/10
SPECIAL CONSIDERATIONS: Lots of narrow stretches, and many bridges to cross. Numbers are capped at 6,000, so early applications are necessary, and book accommodation far in advance.

CONTACT:
Venice Marathon Club
via Linghindal,
5/5-30172 Venezia Mestre
Italy
☎ +39 41 532 18 71
✉ info@venicemarathon.it
🖥 www.venicemarathon.it

Rome Marathon | Italy

For the experience of 'running through history' no other marathon is quite like Rome because it takes in an amazing number of historical landmarks. The Colosseum, Vatican City and the Trevi Fountain are just a few of the delights on offer. These scenic benefits are explained because Rome is saturated with ancient and dramatic landmarks, but also because the centre of the city is closed off for marathon day giving runners the best the city can offer.

RACE DETAILS

WHEN? March
WHEN TO APPLY: October of the year before
HOW MANY TAKE PART? 16,000
DIFFICULTY RATING: 6/10
SPECIAL CONSIDERATIONS: Highly praised for its scenery, but the frequency of cobbled streets might pose problems for some. Bring your own energy gels. Can get congested and hot in places.

CONTACT:
Viale B, Maratona di Roma
Bardanzellu 65,
00155 Roma
Italy
☎ +39 06 40 65064
✉ www.maratonadiroma.it

26

WHILE YOU'RE THERE

Art, beauty, history, and the Italian way of life are all to be found in Rome. There are 500 landmarks along the course, including St Paul's Basilica, the Villa Borghese, the Circus Maximus and the Spanish Steps. **The Colosseum** is everyone's must-see while in Rome, but beware of hawkers dressed in Roman outfits, who'll charge a fortune for a photo. Be wary of tourist traps, for example, in **espresso bars** always stand up to sip your coffee – cafés can charge four times as much if they serve you at a table.

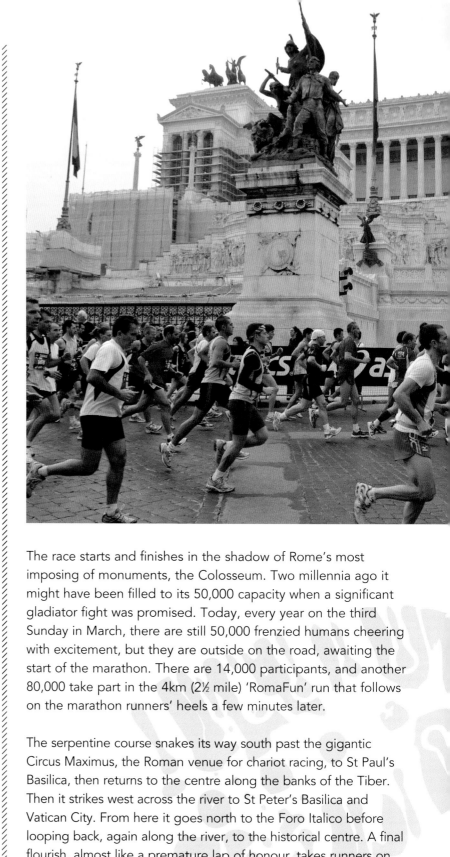

The race starts and finishes in the shadow of Rome's most imposing of monuments, the Colosseum. Two millennia ago it might have been filled to its 50,000 capacity when a significant gladiator fight was promised. Today, every year on the third Sunday in March, there are still 50,000 frenzied humans cheering with excitement, but they are outside on the road, awaiting the start of the marathon. There are 14,000 participants, and another 80,000 take part in the 4km (2½ mile) 'RomaFun' run that follows on the marathon runners' heels a few minutes later.

The serpentine course snakes its way south past the gigantic Circus Maximus, the Roman venue for chariot racing, to St Paul's Basilica, then returns to the centre along the banks of the Tiber. Then it strikes west across the river to St Peter's Basilica and Vatican City. From here it goes north to the Foro Italico before looping back, again along the river, to the historical centre. A final flourish, almost like a premature lap of honour, takes runners on

Previous page: Runners pass through the Piazza del Popolo.

Above: Cobbled streets add to the charm of the old city, but wear cushioned running shoes to avoid very sore legs and feet.

Top right: The Rome Marathon is a perfect tourist marathon, taking in all the ancient sites.

Above right: Reviews have only positive things to say about this well-supported marathon.

a tour of the Piazza del Popolo, the Villa Borghese, the Spanish Steps and the Trevi Fountain. Marathons in other European capitals offer a sprinkling of sights separated by long suburban or commercial stretches, but every step run through the Eternal City brings another twist, another vista, and another marvel.

The weather is generally mild and the course is surprisingly flat, managing to avoid all seven of the hills on which the city is famously built. Fast times have been recorded here, indicating that the cobbled streets around the Colosseum at the start and finish – 2km (1¼ miles) of them to start and 4km (2½ miles) of them to finish – are no impediment.

For marathon runners more than others, all roads lead to Rome. It is fitting to recall that Rome has been the scene of epic sporting events for more than 3,000 years, and the drama of the modern marathon lives up to this legacy.

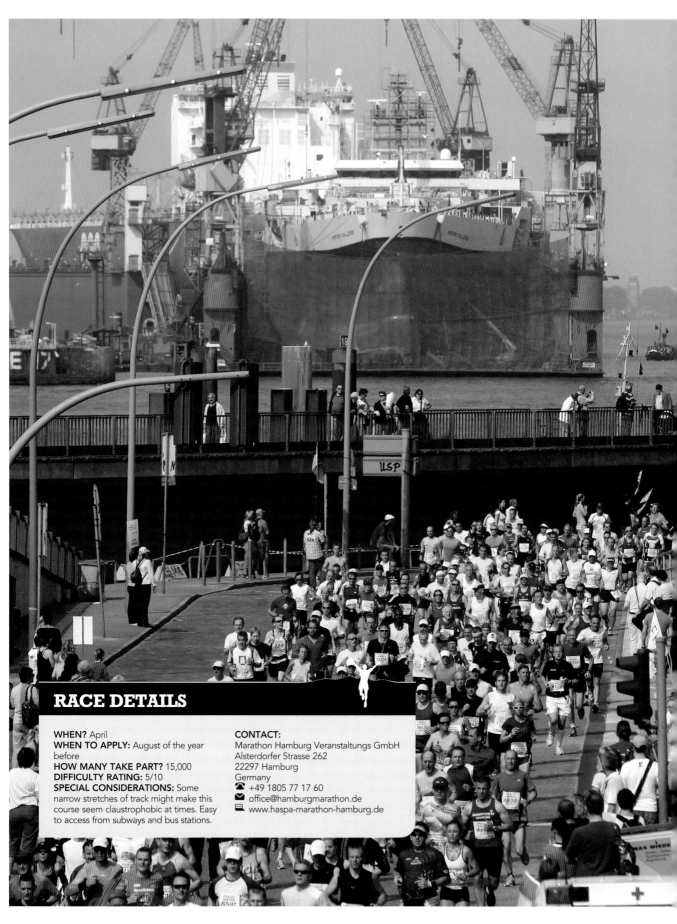

RACE DETAILS

WHEN? April
WHEN TO APPLY: August of the year before
HOW MANY TAKE PART? 15,000
DIFFICULTY RATING: 5/10
SPECIAL CONSIDERATIONS: Some narrow stretches of track might make this course seem claustrophobic at times. Easy to access from subways and bus stations.

CONTACT:
Marathon Hamburg Veranstaltungs GmbH
Alsterdorfer Strasse 262
22297 Hamburg
Germany
☎ +49 1805 77 17 60
✉ office@hamburgmarathon.de
🖥 www.haspa-marathon-hamburg.de

Hamburg Marathon | Germany

This is the city where The Beatles were introduced to the world, and its marathon is just as keen to swing to a different rhythm. Here you'll be swept along with the pounding footsteps of 15,000 marathon runners and the best crowd support of any long-distance race. Cries of 'du schaffst es' (you can do it!) keep runners resolved to the finish.

It is the huge crowds that rally the marathon spirit with enthusiastic supporters blowing whistles, horns and trumpets, or bashing out tempo on pots and pans from their homes overlooking the course. There are an estimated 25 supporters for every one runner, so the race turns into a 42km (26 mile) party. Perhaps the most heartening feature is that the support is at its loudest at the 30km (18 mile) point when many runners need it most.

The first thing that hits you about the Hamburg Marathon is how easy it is to get to. Subway stations stop right beside the starting point. Hamburg ensures all participants are well looked after, with water available every 2.5km (1½ miles) and energy drinks every 5km (3 miles). There are plenty of tubs of water along the course for dipping hats, sponges or anything you want to cool down with.

The course here is flat but tightly packed with runners. Hamburg has been described as Germany's most livable city and you feel something of this in the spirit that flows along the course come marathon day. At the pre-race Expo newcomers can take a bus tour around the course so they can become acquainted with it before the events begin.

Hamburg is one of the biggest ports in Europe with a photogenic city combining docklands, canals, classic market squares, churches and vast lakes. All of these are taken in during the race, as well as the suburbs that most visitors normally don't make the effort to see. The bridges and alleyways that create the atmosphere of this harbour town are all included.

Left: It is customary to finish off proceedings with steines of beer, a sauna or fresh fish from the city's famous seafood market.

WHILE YOU'RE THERE
The city is known as the 'green city of the Elbe' as more than half of the metropolitan area is covered in **green space and parks**. In fact, there are reputed to be more trees than people in this city. By far the most spectacular recent addition to the city landscape is the **Hamburg Opera House**, opened in 2012 and second only in prominence to Sydney's famous landmark. It is more than 325 years since culture-loving Germans had their own opera house in Hamburg. The **Reeperbahn** is great for a night out and for retracing the steps of The Beatles. See: www.hamburg-tourism.de/en

Frankfurt Marathon | Germany

A century ago indoor marathons were an established format – an alternative to the country lanes on which the first marathons were run. During the 1908 London Olympics, the Italian Dorando Pietri was 'assisted' across the finishing line and then disqualified amid great furore in favour of the American Johnny Hayes. Because of the massive public interest in this drama and the re-matches that were touted, a number of indoor marathons were staged as spectacles for enthusiastic crowds who paid high entry fees.

Today, marathons are all about taking over city streets, a stretch of desert, or a Caribbean island to create a dramatic and exhilarating course for runners and spectators alike, but the Frankfurt Marathon harks back to the spirit of these early marathons. The final 100m (328ft) of this city-stomping extravaganza takes runners inside the city's Festival Hall.

Once inside, you'll realise that the venue's name is an appropriate one. As the runners pour in, they are greeted by fireworks, brass bands, and 10,000 spectators. Call it an Oktoberfest high on running, rather than total inebriation. This detail alone makes the race special, turning the atmosphere into something more like a concert, or the opening ceremony at a football match, rather than to other outdoor marathons.

Frankfurt is a business city, with chrome-finished buildings that town planners commissioned to follow the style of the skyline of Manhattan or Chicago. Squint your eyes and you'll see there is a similarity.

WHILE YOU'RE THERE

There is a labyrinth of historical and modern buildings renowned for their artistic wonder. Highlights include the **Städel Institute of Art**, housing paintings from the Middle Ages, and the **Liebighaus**, boasting fine displays of sculpture. Waiting on the other side of the river is the **Museum of Modern Art** and the **Schirn Gallery**. There are a total of 60 museums in Frankfurt, all of which hold internationally acclaimed collections.

Right: The indoor finish along a red carpet provides an unusual finale to the Frankfurt Marathon.

The Frankfurt Marathon attracts about 21,000 participants and 35,000 spectators along the entire route, with around 9,500 running the full distance every year. The course runs in the shadow of the skyscrapers, and takes in other landmarks such as the Italian Renaissance-style Alte Oper – one of Europe's finest opera houses, up until its destruction in 1944, and then, once again, when it was rebuilt and restored to its former glory in 1981. There are also other towering spectacles en route such as the Eschenheimer Turm, a northern gate tower of the former city fortifications, built around 1400 by cathedral master builder, Madern Gerthener.

The architecture, though, is not what the international community comes for. In fact, it is the spectacular indoor finish that has made the Frankfurt marathon something of a legend.

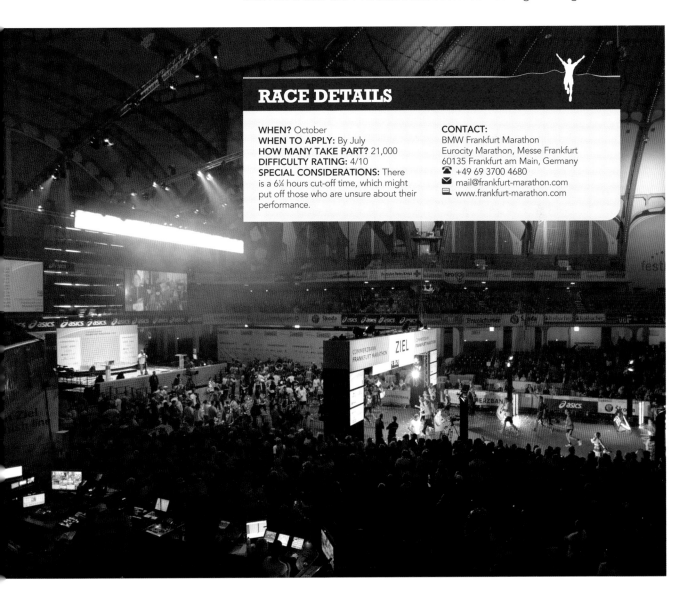

RACE DETAILS

WHEN? October
WHEN TO APPLY: By July
HOW MANY TAKE PART? 21,000
DIFFICULTY RATING: 4/10
SPECIAL CONSIDERATIONS: There is a 6¼ hours cut-off time, which might put off those who are unsure about their performance.

CONTACT:
BMW Frankfurt Marathon
Eurocity Marathon, Messe Frankfurt
60135 Frankfurt am Main, Germany
☎ +49 69 3700 4680
✉ mail@frankfurt-marathon.com
🖥 www.frankfurt-marathon.com

RACE DETAILS

WHEN? September
WHEN TO APPLY: By January
HOW MANY TAKE PART? 4,000
DIFFICULTY RATING: 9/10
SPECIAL CONSIDERATIONS: It is a marathon for the serious contender and unless you have superhero fitness you'll be walking for many of the final stretches. Despite this, there is a 6½ hour cut-off time. Mountain terrain, but water and refreshments are in plentiful supply.

CONTACT:
Jungfrau-Marathon Incoming Office
Strandbadstrasse 44
CH-3800 Interlaken
Switzerland
☎ +41 33 827 62 90
✉ info@jungfrau-marathon.ch
🖥 www.jungfrau-marathon.ch

Jungfrau Marathon |
Switzerland

Jungfrau is a mountain race for the seriously committed, where every few kilometres the challenge changes with increasingly steep gradients to be tackled as you gain altitude and lose oxygen. Rising to the challenge pays off with great views, and the unparalleled feeling of achievement in making it to the finish line.

The event is as much about climbing as it is about running. The race centres around the Kleine Scheidegg, a mountain pass that rises 2,061m (6,762ft) above the Swiss town of Interlaken. The first 25km (15½ miles) are on relatively flat ground and the going is good, but it is in the last 17km (10½ miles) where the real climbing begins and your willpower is tested. Those that rush into an early lead might never make it to the end; it is all about pacing and stamina.

WHILE YOU'RE THERE

Jungfrau's nearest town is **Interlaken**, small enough to get around on foot or bike, and itself a great holiday destination for exploring the **Bernese Oberland**. It is also served by trains to Zurich or Geneva if you want a more metropolitan fix. The town is great for shopping for Swiss souvenirs. For health spa enthusiasts the **Bödelibad Interlaken** has a great sauna, steam bath and whirlpool. See: www.myswitzerland.com

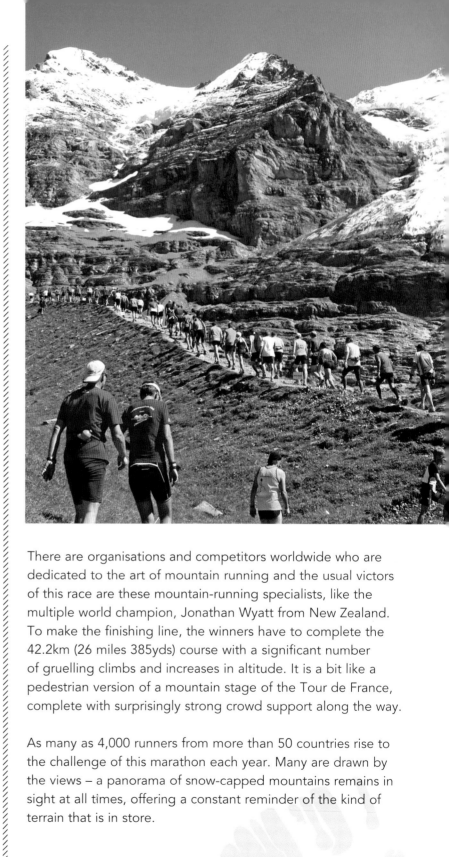

There are organisations and competitors worldwide who are dedicated to the art of mountain running and the usual victors of this race are these mountain-running specialists, like the multiple world champion, Jonathan Wyatt from New Zealand. To make the finishing line, the winners have to complete the 42.2km (26 miles 385yds) course with a significant number of gruelling climbs and increases in altitude. It is a bit like a pedestrian version of a mountain stage of the Tour de France, complete with surprisingly strong crowd support along the way.

As many as 4,000 runners from more than 50 countries rise to the challenge of this marathon each year. Many are drawn by the views – a panorama of snow-capped mountains remains in sight at all times, offering a constant reminder of the kind of terrain that is in store.

Previous page: The spectacular scenery is a delightful bonus in this tough marathon.

Above: The ascents in the Jungfrau Marathon follow a steep gradient, with climbs from the valley bottom to 1,800m (5,900ft).

Top right: Even seasoned marathon runners describe this event as a race of two halves: the first half is a run and the second half is a hike.

Right: A steady stream of runners cross the high points of this scenic run single-file.

Runners pass through Interlaken and then run alongside the wide, refreshing expanse of Lake Brienz, and through mountain villages where crowds enthusiastically applaud the runners. It is smooth going as runners pass onward to the magnificence of the Staubbach Falls, but after 25km (15½ miles) the mountain rises up, and the gruelling fight begins. You must make it up 26 sharp mountain bends before reaching 30km (18½ miles) where music and a cheering crowd help to spur runners onward up the final inclines, beyond the tops of the ski slopes and above the tree line.

From here runners head on to the foot of the Eiger Glacier, and reach the highest point of the race at 2,000m (6,500ft). The finish lies just beyond, from where there is a view of the high alpine peaks, reminding runners why they came in the first place – to absorb the natural beauty of glaciers, rivers and forests, and stand at the finish feeling that they are on top of the world.

RACE DETAILS

WHEN? Mid-October
WHEN TO APPLY: January to September
HOW MANY TAKE PART? 10,000
DIFFICULTY RATING: 4/10
SPECIAL CONSIDERATIONS: One of the fastest courses on the world circuit. Less drama and challenge compared to other marathons.

CONTACT:
TCS Amsterdam Marathon
c/o Le Champion
PO Box 5029
1802 TA Alkmaar, The Netherlands
☎ +31 72 532 48 49
✉ info@tcsamsterdammarathon.nl
🖥 www.tcsamsterdammarathon.nl

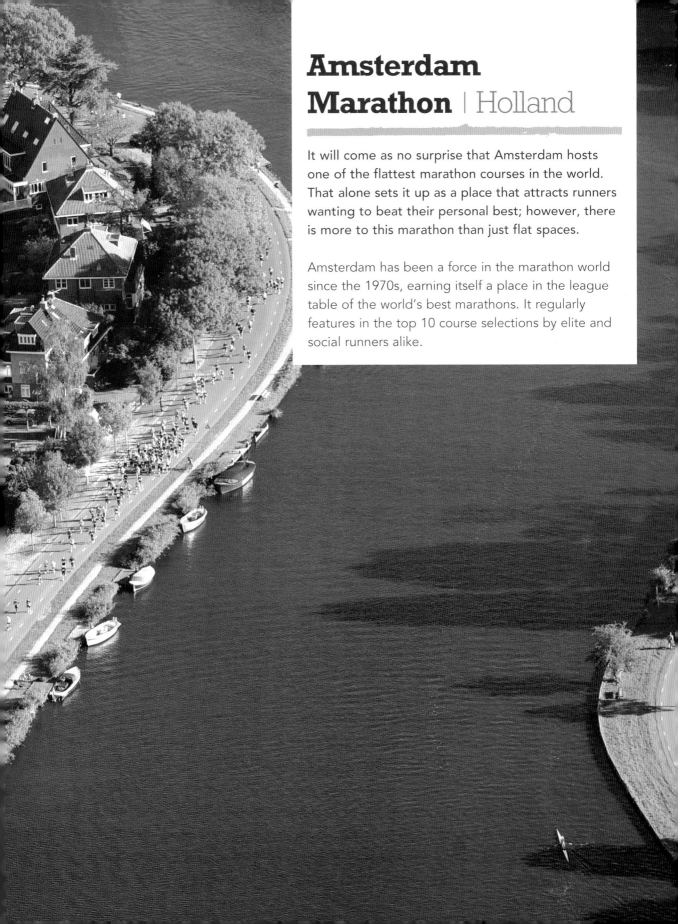

Amsterdam Marathon | Holland

It will come as no surprise that Amsterdam hosts one of the flattest marathon courses in the world. That alone sets it up as a place that attracts runners wanting to beat their personal best; however, there is more to this marathon than just flat spaces.

Amsterdam has been a force in the marathon world since the 1970s, earning itself a place in the league table of the world's best marathons. It regularly features in the top 10 course selections by elite and social runners alike.

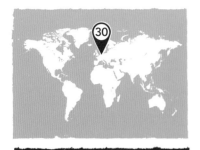

WHILE YOU'RE THERE

You can marvel at the masterpieces at the **Van Gogh Museum**, or see other masters such as Matisse and Picasso at the **Stedelijk Museum**.
The **Red Light District** and its paraded wares and peep shows always draws crowds.
One sight visitors never tire of is the maze of canals, each one lined with a myriad shops, galleries and authentic cafés. The most picturesque of canals is **Prinsengracht**, lined by shady trees and colourful houseboats. Here you'll also find **Anne Frank's House**. A well-kept secret worth visiting is Amsterdam's 14th-century garden at **Begijnhof**. See: www.begijnhofamsterdam.nl

Previous page: The marathon route alongside the Amstel River.

Above: The Mizuno Half Marathon Business Run, the Mizuno 8km (5 mile) run and the 1km (¾ mile) Olympic Kids Run all take place alongside the main event.

Although the course often rewards those that come to run with a fast time and post-marathon bragging rights, only once has the fastest time of the year been set in Amsterdam and that was in the 1928 Olympics. This venue is a run for the amateur, while at the same time offering a world-class course.

Runners from more than 70 countries gather for the start in front of the main stand in the magnificent 1924 Olympic Stadium. The course starts and finishes with a 4km (2½ mile) out-and-back but the 34km (21 miles) in between are made up of one large lap. The 1928 Olympic marathon was Amsterdam's first, and the present-day marathon retraces much of the original course.

During this lap the course meanders through lush greenery to the south of Amsterdam, following the Amstel River from 12–25km (7½–15½ miles). Runners then head back into town past the Amsterdam Arena, the Indische Buurt and through the world famous Vondelpark before returning to finish inside the Olympic Stadium. It is said that the only gradients you'll find are the occasional bridges that cross the famous canals.

For large swathes of the course you'll pass rivers, lakes and the iconic windmills for which the country is famous. The rural setting offers a more refreshing prospect and a better quality of air compared to many other big city marathons. Crowds are strong in Amsterdam and spectators are often on hand to offer water to runners as the course cuts through suburban areas. Elsewhere you will have to rely on the official water stations.

Rock 'n' Roll Madrid Marathon | Spain

Like many other major city marathons the Rock 'n' Roll Madrid Marathon was first dreamed up by a group of sports lovers. It took years to sketch plans, organise a route and turn these dreams into reality. Back in 1978, a mass participation marathon was a new idea to the Spanish people, but they have gradually warmed to it and it has become a source of civic pride and a means to project the identity of their city, as happened so poignantly, and with great force, just five weeks after the 2004 Madrid train bombings. Local runners are always a significant presence but organisers see boosting foreign participation as the key to doubling numbers from the current 10,000 runners to their goal of 20,000.

Madrid lies at an altitude of 670m (2,200ft) – enough to make a difference to your likely finishing time. However, the Spanish spring usually offers good running conditions in a city that can, at other times, be hot and humid. In Madrid, locals venture out on a Saturday night no earlier than 10pm and throng the streets en masse throughout the night with no expectation of returning home until well after first light. This social routine works well for the marathon, which then benefits from the relatively empty streets from which runners can strike out on their early-morning mission. The start and finish lie right in the heart of the city on those just-vacated streets.

From the start line runners tackle a long, gentle incline northward. This is the part of the course on which to relax, mindful that undue effort at even this slight altitude will probably rebound on you later in the race. These early kilometres are along wide avenues, but bereft of any engaging urban detail. The field of runners thins out slowly, and by the time participants approach the half marathon distance there is enough room to look around.

WHILE YOU'RE THERE

For some great sightseeing go to the Metro by La Latina Station. From there take a stroll around **Plaza de la Cebada**, **Cava Baja** and **Plaza de la Paja**. After 9pm the streets slowly come to life. Walk from **el Viaducto Bridge** in the southern limit of La Latina to Plaza España by the **Palacio Real de Madrid**. Alternatively you can sit and feast at the great tapas bars by **Mercado de San Miguel**.

RACE DETAILS

WHEN? April
WHEN TO APPLY: November of the year before
HOW MANY TAKE PART? 10,000
DIFFICULTY RATING: 7/10
SPECIAL CONSIDERATIONS: Course throws up a lot of hills that can challenge the beginner. The city is poised on a dry plain 700m (2,300ft) above sea level, so best to acclimatise to this environment a few days before.

CONTACT:
☎ +858 450 6510 (USA)
✉ rnrmadrid@competitorgroup.com
🖳 www.maratonmadrid.org

Left: The starting line features marathon runners as well as those taking on the challenge of the 10km race, the two run simultaneously.

Above: The race is downhill except for two blocks of 6km (6 miles), each of which include quite steep climbs.

Far right: Madrid is considered a tough marathon with a challenging course, even by seasoned veterans.

Cobbled roads underfoot may inhibit runners from enjoying the surroundings, but there is indeed plenty to see. Competitors sweep into the Puerta del Sol and take a turn past the Plaza Mayor and the Palacio Real. These are the architectural riches of a city which was capital to an empire that covered half the globe. Shortly afterwards runners experience a different ambience, as they descend to the River Manzanares and take in a loop through Madrid's major green space, the Casa de Campo. Here all is serene and peaceful, far from the cheering crowd. The other of Madrid's parks, Retiro, is where the race finishes – runners enter through the grand gateway and have an equally grand finishing straight where spectators bask in the sunshine and await the arrival of their loved one. In Madrid this usually means the father, as the race is predominantly local and over-whelmingly male. Only 6 per cent of the field are women, and this presents the most obvious possible growth area for the future.

Those that run Madrid are drawn back to its espirito de vida. The turnout is impressive and the support comes with passion and intensity that is both a reflection of its people and testimony to the future of this race.

Paris Marathon | France

Although the Arc de Triomphe was built with another kind of triumphalism in mind, it is a fitting centrepiece that dominates both the start and finish area of the Paris Marathon, reminding the thronging crowds just how big a personal victory running a marathon can be. Just getting to the start line on the Champs-Elysées, with the Arc de Triomphe as a backdrop represents a victory of sorts – it is one of the few days of the year that the choking Parisian traffic is held at bay for the benefit of the general public. The grand boulevards of Paris unroll in front of the runners, who for the first 2km (1¼ miles) descend to the Place de La Concorde, and soon afterward reach the Jardin des Tuileries and the Musée du Louvre.

Of the 40,000 runners who take part, more than a quarter come from outside France from 80 different countries. By far the largest group are the British, who flock to the event under the English Channel on Eurostar trains. In a display of entente cordiale, giant flags line the route – Le Tricolore, the Union Jack and the Stars and Stripes abound in an explosion of red, white and blue as if they are welcoming back returning heroes.

In the first Paris Marathon back in 1977 only 87 people finished the race. During the first European running boom of the 1980s numbers swelled to 7,000, but in 1991 the race was called off due to disputes within the race organisation. Since then the Marie de Paris (the city council) have used the Tour de France organisers to stage the race, and it has grown in both size and stature as a result.

The Paris Marathon is central to the city. The start and finish of the race are easily accessed on foot from a host of metro stations, and the course offers a comprehensive tour of the city's sights. If runners have time to glance left as they head down the Rue de Rivoli they will see the Place Vendôme and the ornate Paris Opera in full view.

WHILE YOU'RE THERE

One of the most charming Parisian districts is **Montmarte**, always full of tourists, but still blessed with a village-like atmosphere. It retains the flavour for which Paris is famous. Packed with cafés and alleys, it is the inspiration for many paintings from the artists who lived there during the 19th and 20th centuries. These include Edgar Degas, Henri Matisse, Henri de Toulouse-Lautrec, Pierre-Auguste Renoir, and Pablo Picasso. Go to Montmarte's famous **cemetery** and you'll see many are buried there. For a more life-affirming experience **Le Moulin Rouge** still swings to cabaret.

Right: The Paris Marathon offers a scenic route, taking in all the major landmarks of this city – however bottlenecks can occur.

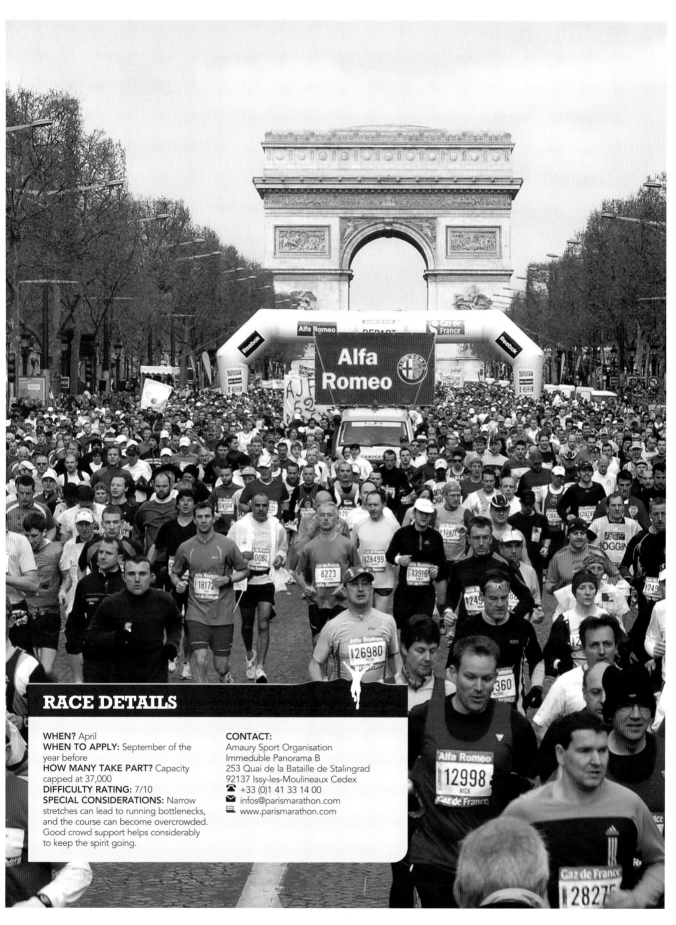

RACE DETAILS

WHEN? April
WHEN TO APPLY: September of the year before
HOW MANY TAKE PART? Capacity capped at 37,000
DIFFICULTY RATING: 7/10
SPECIAL CONSIDERATIONS: Narrow stretches can lead to running bottlenecks, and the course can become overcrowded. Good crowd support helps considerably to keep the spirit going.

CONTACT:
Amaury Sport Organisation
Immeduble Panorama B
253 Quai de la Bataille de Stalingrad
92137 Issy-les-Moulineaux Cedex
☎ +33 (0)1 41 33 14 00
✉ infos@parismarathon.com
🖥 www.parismarathon.com

The wedding-cake style Hôtel de Ville is a little further along on the right before runners reach the Place de La Bastille. Just beyond, as runners approach the Bois de Vincennes, a giant banner proclaims 'Courage: only 32km (20 miles) to go'. After a serpentine tour of the Bois, in which spectators are sparse and the mood almost bucolic, the race passes the halfway point and hits the Rive Droite of the River Seine at 23km (14¼ miles). The north embankment is not quite flat; runners are sometimes diverted below underpasses in order to avoid closing the bridges down. Surfacing from one such dip, you will catch a glimpse of Notre Dame, then a few kilometres later, at 29km (18 miles), you emerge to find the Eiffel Tower rearing up on your left-hand side.

The course takes a detour around the Parc des Princes rugby stadium and the Roland Garros tennis clay courts before entering the Bois de Boulogne at 36km (22½ miles). The last 6km (3¾ miles) of the course are in the Bois, and largely devoid of crowd support. This makes the final 200m (656ft) sprint down the Avenue Foch all the more of a climactic moment and the finish gantry your own personal Arc de Triomphe.

Right: Paris rightly attracts thousands to its marathon, which takes in all the sightseeing scenery that the city has to offer.

Below: Times are not fast for this tricky marathon, and cobblestones add to the challenge for some runners.

RACE DETAILS

WHEN? March
WHEN TO APPLY: By January of the same year
HOW MANY TAKE PART? 15,000
DIFFICULTY RATING: 5/10
SPECIAL CONSIDERATIONS: Mild weather conditions at this time of year, low humidity, hills at the beginning and end. Good carnival atmosphere.

CONTACT:
Zurich Marató de Barcelona
Gran Via 8-10, 6ª planta
08902 Hospitalet de Llobregat
Barcelona, Spain
☎ +34 902 43 17 63
✉ info@zurichmaratobarcelona.es
🖥 www.zurichmaratobarcelona.es

Barcelona Marathon | Spain

Hosting the 1992 Olympic Games gave Barcelona an enduring international sporting profile in the world. The Games and their legacy brought a wave of construction to the city's sports facilities and an awareness of how positive energy can renew the spirit of a city, and its sports prowess. Having more recently hosted the European Athletics Championship has helped to improve the infrastructure further, making Barcelona an excellent marathon venue.

The Barcelona Marathon was established in 1978, in a way that has become a familiar model – a Spaniard had run in the New York City Marathon and was so impressed that he returned home to set about creating one in Barcelona. This untried event was then consigned to a route outside town for its inaugural edition to avoid disrupting normal city life, but even so it attracted 1,050 runners and double that the following year. The course was adapted for the 1980 version when it was held within the city and received far more attention. The race impressed Mayor Pasqual Maragall who decided to launch an Olympic bid on the back of its success.

In the 1980s Barcelona made some innovations to their marathon that have become part of the modern standard – in 1983 they were the first to introduce dope testing, and one of the first to use an electrically powered lead vehicle. Even so, the number of runners only edged up slowly until Olympic year, when 6,000 finished on a tough course that would then be used for the Olympic Marathon a few months later.

After the Olympics, the 'Marato', though not the city, slipped back to its former level. Tensions between the club organisation and the city authorities eventually led to the cancellation of the 2005 race and the commissioning of the organisers of the Tour de France to stage the 2006 race on a route once again located entirely within the city. Since 2006, entries have risen significantly, surpassing 10,000 in 2010 and now in excess of 15,000. Foreign runners make up a significant proportion.

Left: A beautiful course with many famous landmarks as well as the Mediterranean sea.

WHILE YOU'RE THERE

It is **Antonio Gaudi's architecture** that many visitors come to see, but few venture out to **Parc Güell**. This is where the artist used to live, and it hosts a wonderland of his more ambitious mosaics and architectural imaginings. The park makes a refreshing alternative to **Las Ramblas** which has become more of a tourist trap than a place to experience the real Barcelona. The Parc boasts fairytale sculptures and grand staircases. There is a museum about the life of the man who has become synonymous with the Catalan capital. Also venture out to the nearby town of **Girona** and its surroundings.

The Marato provides a fitting vehicle through which visitors can catch the sights and sounds of city life that have made Barcelona one of Europe's favourite destinations. Starting at the Plaça d'Espanya, runners pass through the Eixample district, and close by Barcelona Football Club's Camp Nou stadium, the Torre Agbar, Port Olímpic, and along the city's most renowned street, the Ramblas. The stunning architecture of Antonio Gaudi intermittently looms over the route like giant blocks of melted candle wax. The monumental Sagrada Familia cathedral, as well as some smaller apartment buildings, enliven the route with a quirky grandeur.

Barcelona's artisan culture is showcased at 24 different points along the route where music, art and crafts create a carnival flavour while the race is in full swing. This lends a vibrancy and warmth to a marathon that is rapidly building a following worthily in tune with this iconic city.

Right: The Sagrada Familia cathedral by Gaudi is one of the landmarks of the race.

Below: La Pedrera, a residential building with undulating stone walls and a UNESCO World Heritage Site.

London Marathon | UK

Like many Great British inventions, the London Marathon was dreamt up in a pub over a pint of beer. Athletes and founders Chris Brasher and John Disley modelled it after visiting the New York Marathon in 1979. The festival atmosphere and a route that embraced the key landmarks of one of the world's great cities were essential ingredients. From the launch year in 1981 when 7,000 ran, the participants more than doubled to 16,000 by 1982, making it bigger than the New York event it set out to emulate. Since then numbers have crept up to 35,000.

Back in the 1970s, long-distance running was a lonely pursuit. Runners were usually consigned to trudging through fields with only cows as spectators. The London Marathon project aimed to gather these lonely joggers and get them to take part in a celebratory spectacle like that of New York's, which had been referred to by Chris Brasher as 'The World's Most Human Race'. He explained that what he had seen demonstrated that 'the human race can be one joyous family, working together, laughing together and achieving the impossible'. He and Disley set out to achieve that 'impossibility' in London.

34

WHILE YOU'RE THERE

Try some traditional UK carb-laden fare and have some **fish and chips**. A favourite is Poppies, near Spitalfields market. The eatery is decked out in 1950s vintage diner décor, and comes to life late on Sunday evenings. To fit in some sight-seeing, one of the quickest ways to see London is to take one of the speedy Clipper river boats that covers many key sites from **Richmond** to **Big Ben**, as well as the marathon starting point at **Greenwich maritime centre**. With a day pass you can hop on and off as many times as you want. See: www.thamesclippers.com and www.thamesflyer.com

Left: The wheelchair event at the London Marathon attracts a world-class field.

Right: The London Marathon has a fabulous atmosphere as thousands take to the streets to raise money for charities of all kinds.

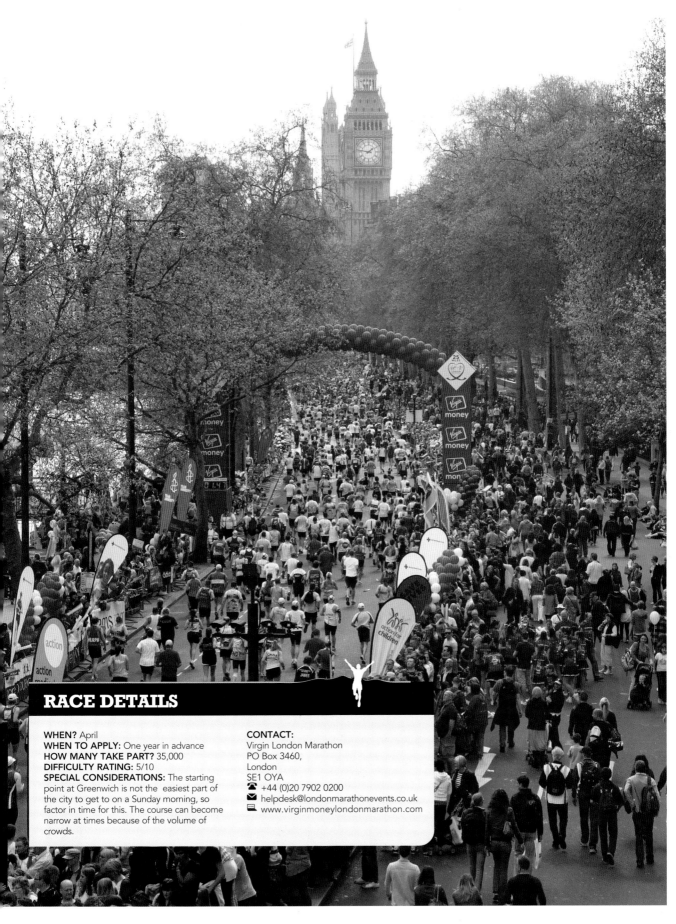

RACE DETAILS

WHEN? April
WHEN TO APPLY: One year in advance
HOW MANY TAKE PART? 35,000
DIFFICULTY RATING: 5/10
SPECIAL CONSIDERATIONS: The starting point at Greenwich is not the easiest part of the city to get to on a Sunday morning, so factor in time for this. The course can become narrow at times because of the volume of crowds.

CONTACT:
Virgin London Marathon
PO Box 3460,
London
SE1 OYA
☎ +44 (0)20 7902 0200
✉ helpdesk@londonmarathonevents.co.uk
🖨 www.virginmoneylondonmarathon.com

The course has kept to essentially the same route, starting in the ornate gardens and 17th-century grandeur of Greenwich, a host site to events of the 2012 Olympic Games, before dropping down to the River Thames at Woolwich and then turning up river towards Tower Bridge. This iconic Victorian structure is almost at the halfway mark, acting as a gateway to the rest of the course as runners head back down river toward the Canary Wharf business district and many of London's tallest buildings. The course then loops back toward Tower Bridge and the Tower of London and goes on to the Embankment, passing Cleopatra's Needle, and reaching Big Ben, from where there is less than 1.5km (1 mile) to run. The finishing line comes 200m (656ft) after runners pass directly in front of Buckingham Palace.

One thing that the founding fathers may not have foreseen was the way in which the London Marathon has become such an effective and high-profile vehicle for charitable fundraising. With the race so over-subscribed, one way of securing a place is to raise funds for a charity that offers guaranteed places. This has generated vast sums (estimated at £50 million, or US $80 million, each year). It creates a unique atmosphere of cajoling money from bystanders as well as mammoth personal efforts from particpants who are often dressed in outrageous costumes.

Above: The London Marathon is so over-subscribed that it can take up to six years to secure a place in the ballot. Running for a charity is another way to get you in.

Loch Ness Marathon | Scotland

The Loch Ness Marathon logo, a sinuous shoelace snaking through running shoe eyelets, is worthy of the famous monster it depicts. It is as close as you will come to spotting 'Nessie', and the organisers do not attempt to pretend otherwise. Loch Ness, however, has other more tangible attractions.

Inverness is a long way north in Scotland, although its airport has good connections with other UK airports. Perhaps because of this northerly location the town provides a warm welcome. Part of this involves the local whiskies from which the area derives as much fame as the elusive monster. However, for runners the most immediate impression is that of the serene landscape. Inverness is an imposing blend of granite brick and modern office blocks, but this is where the race ends – the point-to-point course starts on an appropriately rugged, unadorned stretch of road to which runners are taken by bus on race morning and which takes on the look of a latter-day gathering of lycra-clad clans.

Belying the serenity of today's quiet glens, clan feuding dominated life here 300 years ago. Inverness was sacked seven times and Bonnie Prince Charlie's forces were crushed on Culloden Field in the last bloody battle ever fought on British soil. You can now view the site of the famous battle at Culloden Moor Visitors Centre. The marathon is a less bloodthirsty affair, but the ambition for victory could be said to be just as strong.

As the dawn light spreads maybe something of the past can be sensed, but race preparation leaves little time for diversion. The sounds of bagpipes and drums rouse runners to the starting line but, once on the road, the only traffic you're likely to encounter are fellow runners, red squirrels, deer and eagles. The course begins by passing through farmland on side roads before steering toward the side of the Loch. The route drops from start to finish, although there are also some uphill sections. The first 10km (6 miles) are gentle, sheltered by woods with scenic views regularly opening up across the Loch. Villages and spectators dot the route, offering refreshments to the weary.

WHILE YOU'RE THERE

You won't have time to take in the full beauty of **Loch Ness** during the marathon. Take a cruise along the loch and stop off at **Urquhart Castle** while you're touring. The edifice makes an imposing backdrop to this corner of the lake. Further afield you're in the prime vicinity to take some **whisky distillery tours**, many of which offer free tastings. The nearby town of **Inverness** makes a great spot for an afternoon stroll. See www.visitscotland.com and www.spiritofspeyside.com

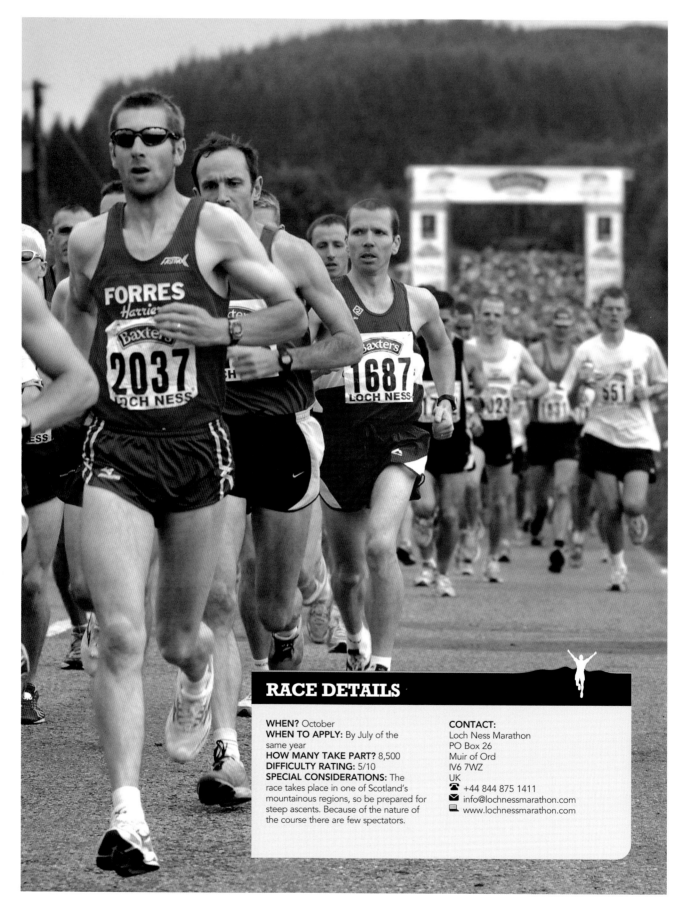

RACE DETAILS

WHEN? October
WHEN TO APPLY: By July of the same year
HOW MANY TAKE PART? 8,500
DIFFICULTY RATING: 5/10
SPECIAL CONSIDERATIONS: The race takes place in one of Scotland's mountainous regions, so be prepared for steep ascents. Because of the nature of the course there are few spectators.

CONTACT:
Loch Ness Marathon
PO Box 26
Muir of Ord
IV6 7WZ
UK
☎ +44 844 875 1411
✉ info@lochnessmarathon.com
🖥 www.lochnessmarathon.com

Organisers have strategically placed lone bagpipers in places where they suspect morale might flag: for example, when runners have left the Loch behind and head toward the town. Once the River Ness Bridge has been crossed and runners double back on themselves along the river they are likely to be able to sense the finish. Long-term sponsor, Baxter's Foods, offers participants hearty Scottish fare to replenish runners' spent resources once they reach the race finish.

Between the natural scenery, clean fresh air and warmth of the local hospitality, it is not so surprising that this relatively secluded corner of the British Isles attracts a sell-out field, with runners coming from 30 countries for a chance to race in this remote, romantic Highland location. Off the track, the Loch Ness area is one of Europe's richest areas for natural bounty, thriving with exotic birds, red deer and the humble goat. One of its most recent additions is the opening of the South Loch Ness walking trail which helps visitors see some of the best points of the loch that have not been open before.

Sahara Marathon |
Algeria

To run through territory as forbidding as the Sahara requires a certain resolve, but that pales into insignificance compared to what lies behind the creation of this event. The race was conceived as a humanitarian initiative to raise awareness of living conditions in the Western Sahara. Marathon participants discover these easily enough: for several days they are billeted in refugee camps within the homes of the displaced Sahrawi and, as a result, discover the culture around them.

RACE DETAILS

WHEN? October
WHEN TO APPLY: Preparations and applications should be made one year in advance
HOW MANY TAKE PART? 400
DIFFICULTY RATING: 9/10
SPECIAL CONSIDERATIONS: Like no other marathon, so throw away all preconceptions. Running through the desert can be testing, but there are plenty of water stations, and the crowd support is great at stopover camps, not to mention the hospitality.

CONTACT:

✉ rmdurli@saharawi.org
🖥 www.saharamarathon.org (the website includes contacts for individual countries)

36

WHILE YOU'RE THERE

The race takes place near the town of **Tindouf**, well worth exploring for its friendly faces, camels, and whitewash street buildings. The desert's cape is also good for photography and the more adventurous pastime of **jeep overlanding**, A word of caution, however; always go with a trusted guide, as landmines pose a threat, as well as the danger of being in the desert too long. Many marathon runners stay **in the camps** with the friends they have made on the way, once the race is over.

Previous page: The Sahara Marathon demands greater participation of its runners than most marathons. The 500 entrants stay as guests in the tents of the Sahrawi people for one week.

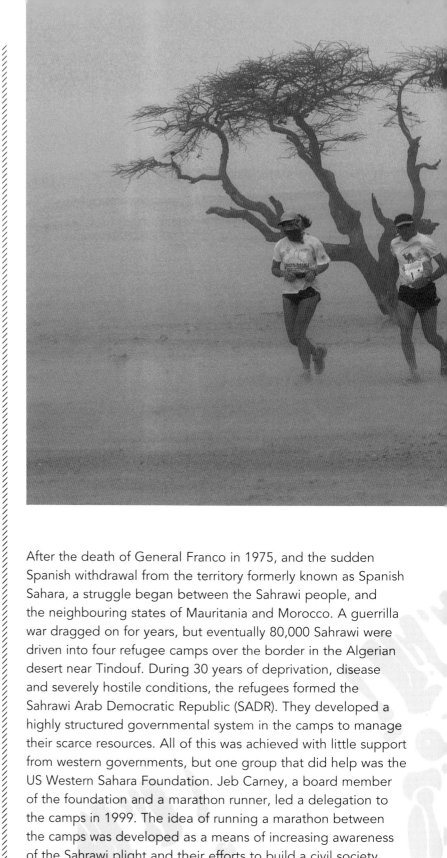

After the death of General Franco in 1975, and the sudden Spanish withdrawal from the territory formerly known as Spanish Sahara, a struggle began between the Sahrawi people, and the neighbouring states of Mauritania and Morocco. A guerrilla war dragged on for years, but eventually 80,000 Sahrawi were driven into four refugee camps over the border in the Algerian desert near Tindouf. During 30 years of deprivation, disease and severely hostile conditions, the refugees formed the Sahrawi Arab Democratic Republic (SADR). They developed a highly structured governmental system in the camps to manage their scarce resources. All of this was achieved with little support from western governments, but one group that did help was the US Western Sahara Foundation. Jeb Carney, a board member of the foundation and a marathon runner, led a delegation to the camps in 1999. The idea of running a marathon between the camps was developed as a means of increasing awareness of the Sahrawi plight and their efforts to build a civil society.

Above: Hard-packed sand is a runner-friendly surface – only when the wind gets up does it present real difficulty.

Top right: A children's race follows the marathon.

Above right: This is a desert run where conditions can be extreme.

The basic idea was simple and, due to the willingness of the Sahrawi, immediately effective. The course was marked out using cairns, or stacks of stones, to guide runners over the open desert between the three refugee camps of El Aaiún, El Aoserd and Smara, each named after an equivalent settlement in Western Sahara. The first marathon was held on 26 February 2001, the 25th anniversary of the founding of SADR.

The first two years of the Sahara Marathon brought in more than 900 runners from 30 countries on charter flights, revealing a glimpse of life in the Sahara that would change their perception of the Sahrawi forever. Participants are hosted during their stay by Sahrawi families, living in their tents and eating with them, experiencing their life and the harsh conditions in the camps. It is a chance to share part of their life, to learn about them, and to create ties that in many cases last for years, with some runners returning every year to run and to see their host families and friends again.

RACE DETAILS

WHEN? Mid April
WHEN TO APPLY: By April of the same year
HOW MANY TAKE PART? 3,000+
DIFFICULTY RATING: 8/10
SPECIAL CONSIDERATIONS: The marathon route in Connemara is entirely paved but very hilly. The weather of this locale is quite unpredictable, so it is best to keep an eye on the forecast closer to race day; dress as if it is going to be cold and wet, with layers that can be removed if the day turns sunny.

CONTACT:
Connemara Marathon Ltd
10 Rathlao
Cartur Mor, Knocknacarra, Galway
Ireland
☎ 087 7526493
✉ info@connemarathon.com
🖥 www.connemarathon.com

Connemara International Marathon | Ireland

Set in the wild west of Ireland, the Connemara International Marathon is one of the world's most spectacular events. While taking in the most breath-taking scenery that Ireland has to offer, international runners and walkers will enjoy a warm Irish welcome and the close sense of comradeship unique to the event as they follow the route along the 'Wild Atlantic Way'.

The 'Connemarathon' is run in April with the half, full and ultra marathon (63km/39 miles) attracting both novice and elite runners and walkers from every corner of the world. The route offers a variety of spectacular land forms: travelling along rugged hills, the Twelve Pins mountain range; stunning glacial lakes and the great expanse of Killary Lough. Runners progress through the sleepy village of Leenane, around the Maam Turk Mountains and up the 'hell of the west' to Maam Cross. There is an unmistakable buzz throughout the day. No other event sends people away with such a taste of Ireland and its highlights. The ultra marathon was added in 2004 and has proved a great success offering a new challenge to those runners who seek to relive the Connemarathon experience.

From modest beginnings with a field of only 72 runners in 2002, the race sells out to capacity and currently accepts more than 3,000 participants. Located in a relatively remote part of the country, the race organisers have to be active in making accommodation and travel suggestions and arranging bus transfers from the major nearby towns to the start line and back again to cater to the many visitors.

If a picture tells a thousand words, then the story you can get from just a glimpse of the Connemarathon website is a long one. Even if you normally find moving images anathema to gleaning the information that you need, you will probably still find the slow panning shots of the Connemara countryside worth studying with full attention.

Left: At the start of the full marathon on April 12, 2015, participants run alongside the stunning Lough Inagh Lake, with the breathtaking Twelve Pins mountain range in the distance.

WHILE YOU'RE THERE

Connemara, considered the real emerald of Ireland, is a beautiful, unspoilt landscape that has much to offer any sportsman or leisure seeker. Experience the majesty of Ireland's mountains and shores from the back of a **Connemara pony** or spend the day golfing, rock climbing, or watching a **Gaelic football match**. For a touch of culture, investigate the megalithic stones, tombs, and castles that litter the nearby countryside.

Right: An Mam Failte: welcome to the village of Maam, part of the scenic route that participants run through.

Far right: The stunning mountain range of the Twelve Pins is a dominant feature on the Connemarathon course.

The race's backdrop consists of snow-topped peaks, partially swathed with deep green conifer forest and with lower slopes covered by wild porcupine grass leading down to icy still lakes. The race organisers cleverly contrived a shoe-shaped logo for their event which references all these elements.

You see runners crossing the finish line looking exhausted yet elated, their happiness evident to all. 'The Run of Your Life' is a very big claim for any race to make about itself – although many among those featured in this book make it – but in this case the assertion is true. Without a doubt you will return home with the feeling of having finished one of the world's truly magical marathons.

Reykjavik Marathon | Iceland

Iceland is far from being the forbidding place that its name might suggest. The Icelandic summer is short, but it offers relatively mild and breezy weather. This, along with often flat, well-surfaced roads and a sparse population, makes it an almost idyllic setting for distance running.

Like the town itself, Reykjavik Marathon lives up to its reputation of being intimate and unpretentious. People often describe the capital as a cosmopolitan city crammed into the form of a fishing village. When the marathon first started just 214 competitors signed up, but that is something that distinguishes this country from anywhere else – life is lived on a smaller (and arguably a more comfortable) scale. The same applies to its marathon. The population of Iceland is a mere 320,000, so anything that attracts overseas visitors usually gains the support of the Icelanders. In their own unfussy way they are very welcoming people.

The focal point of the marathon and the concurrently run half marathon is a picturesque pond called Tjörnin, just outside the city centre on which the Reykjavik City Hall is located. This idyllic setting is a haven full of birdlife and fringed with the distinctive wooden houses that characterise Icelandic domestic architecture. The run begins and ends here, but embraces quite another world in between.

Runners leave the centre almost as soon as they depart from the start line, threading their way through the suburban surroundings and onto the Reykjavik peninsula's coastal path. The imposing green bulk of Mount Esja dominates the landscape from across the bay, still crowned by remnants of snow. Runners turn back toward the city centre, along a route lapped by a geothermally heated beach, another of Iceland's natural wonders.

The natural environment wonderfully complements the running experience in Iceland. Reykjavik translates as 'smoky bay', even though there is no smoke or pollution.

WHILE YOU'RE THERE

The **fishing harbours** are a great place to pick up the latest fresh fish dish. Near the capital there are a myriad of **natural thermal springs**, heated by the underlying thermal rock, making a great antidote to aches and pains resulting from a hard run. The most famous and accessible from the capital is the **Blue Lagoon**. Its springs are made of seawater that come from deep within the earth, capturing minerals that result in bathing waters of around 37°C (98°F) that are renowned for their healing powers. See: ww.bluelagoon.com

Right: Marathoners and half marathoners run the same race, with those doing the shorter distance branching off at 19km (12 miles).

The ancient Viking name refers to the geothermal steam that mysteriously seeps out of the ground. Nonetheless, the air quality is the best in Europe, so visiting runners can breathe easily. They can also enjoy a long relaxing post-race soak in one of Iceland's many geothermal pools. One of them, the 'Blue Lagoon' lies en route to Keflavik International Airport.

Making it to Iceland is an adventure in itself, even if you don't run the marathon. The participants from Europe and North America and beyond have saved money, begged for charity donations and trained hard to be here. You can feel that such investment energises and enthuses the crowd as the starting gun fires.

One reason why Reykjavik Marathon has become such a big event is that it coincides with 'Culture Night', which was created to celebrate the best Icelandic traditions including music, art, and gourmet whaleshark meat-tasting sessions. The programme of events includes string quartets, art exhibits and theatre, while the crowd is a heady mix of graffiti artists and those wearing rock outfits. The marathon after-party culminates with a mammoth firework display, which is the cue to head for the city's clubs and bars. Still riding high from the euphoria of the marathon, participants throw themselves into the all-night party.

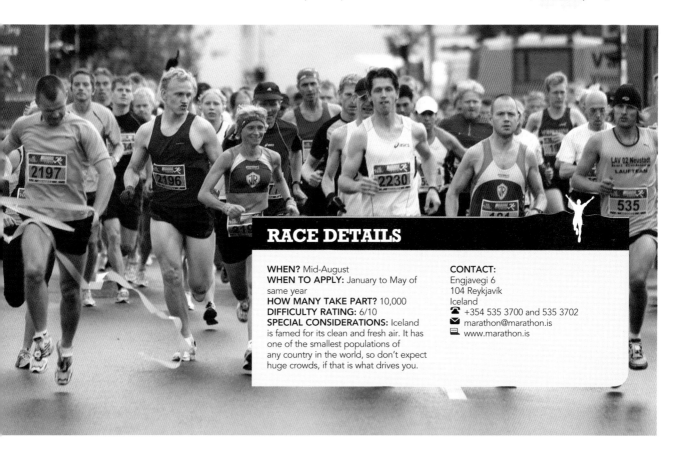

RACE DETAILS

WHEN? Mid-August
WHEN TO APPLY: January to May of same year
HOW MANY TAKE PART? 10,000
DIFFICULTY RATING: 6/10
SPECIAL CONSIDERATIONS: Iceland is famed for its clean and fresh air. It has one of the smallest populations of any country in the world, so don't expect huge crowds, if that is what drives you.

CONTACT:
Engjavegi 6
104 Reykjavík
Iceland
☎ +354 535 3700 and 535 3702
✉ marathon@marathon.is
💻 www.marathon.is

RACE DETAILS

WHEN? July
WHEN TO APPLY: January
HOW MANY TAKE PART? 4,000
DIFFICULTY RATING: 6/10
SPECIAL CONSIDERATIONS: Flat
course, so don't expect huge challenges,
the traffic can be daunting for some.

CONTACT:
Rua Felix Pacheco 150 Bldg C Apt. 102
Leblon 22450 080, Brazil
☎ +21 22 23 2273
✉ maratonadorio@
maratonadorio.com.br
🖥 www.maratonadorio.com.br

Rio de Janeiro Marathon | Brazil

Rio de Janeiro's marathon follows a point-to-point route starting from the western edge of town at Recreio dos Bandeirantes, a strip of development lying between the beach and the inland lagoons and marshes. Runners follow the coast all the way into the city centre. Half-marathon runners start closer to town, at São Conrado. It is after this point that runners encounter a sustained rise as the road climbs around a rocky headland on Oscar Niemeyer Drive. To the right, runners can gaze out over the brilliant blue of the South Atlantic Ocean, while a steep tree-covered cliff rises up on their other side. Around the headland, the road drops back down to beach level about 25km (15½ miles) into the race, and on the beaches themselves Brazilian life is all around to see.

Brazilians treat the beach like people elsewhere would a park, coming to play chess, football or volleyball, chat and meet up with friends – anything rather than just lie around topping up their tans. Each beach has its own distinctive character: upscale Leblon, fashionable Ipanema and popular Copacabana.

Brazil is a country where the spirit of participation is infectious: rogue roller bladers, cyclists and pedestrians will try to join in the marathon. To stop them becoming too involved a lead flotilla of cars and security bikes steer them away and the sound of their sirens clear a path for the oncoming leaders of the race. This happens twice in succession, as Brazilian races commonly feature a separate start for the faster women ahead of the mass field so that leading women can focus on the competition.

From the moment runners reach Leblon the road is flat and the running becomes easy. After the beaches, the route heads inland, cutting through a tunnel to Botafogo Bay. With no attached beach, crowds are thin on the ground here as runners sweep around the bay under the shadow of the Sugar Loaf Mountain towards Flamengo Beach. Runners stay on the highway inland from the beach park, turning at the far end and doubling back to the finish line. It has been a long journey to get here, and even on this midwinter date in mid-July, the day is bound to be hot. No matter, the beach is close at hand.

WHILE YOU'RE THERE

There are few better ways to soak up the native **Carioca** lifestyle than an afternoon on the beach – it is where Brazilian social life is in full force. The more fashionable sands are at **Leblon** or **Ipanema**, rather than **Copacabana**. The **Christ the Redeemer** statue is a must-visit, as is the **Sugar Loaf Mountain**. If you're in need of a post-marathon feast, head to a **churrascaria** (steakhouse), such as Parcão Rio (www.porcao.com.br); hunks of prime steak will be carved onto your plate. There is an amazing salad bar, too, packed with exotic fruit and salads.

If you have a week or more, head to the retreat of **Búzios**, with 30 beaches to choose from.

Left: Spectacular scenery offers a superb backdrop to the physical efforts of the runners.

Standard Chartered Bank Stanley Marathon | Falkland Islands

SCB Stanley Marathon proudly claims to be the most southerly internationally-certified marathon in the world. The Falkland Islands are a British Overseas Territory located at 52 degrees south in the Atlantic Ocean not far north of the southernmost tip of the Americas land mass, Cape Horn. Lying 480km (300 miles) from the Patagonian coast of Argentina, the Islands are exposed to Atlantic gales and the weather is unpredictable.

Race instructions advise: 'The March date has been chosen in the hope that the summer winds will have died down but the temperature not dropped too much. Running into the wind can be particularly uncomfortable'. With true Falklander understatement they add: 'It is unlikely that the race will be cancelled due to the weather but if it is especially bad the start may be briefly delayed.'

The course makes use of all the surfaced roads available. These extend only a short distance from the island capital before becoming stony tracks. Runners start and finish in Stanley, next to the island's only bank and the Town Hall, and run three separate out-and-back sections, repeating the first two of these again before finishing.

Runners first head west along the south shore of Stanley Harbour to the 'Beaver Hangar' – named for a type of seaplane rather than the animal. Looping back, runners return to Stanley centre though residential streets until dropping back down to the waterfront before reaching the war memorial – the last war here was the conflict with Argentina in 1982 – and the Governor's residence.

The course then continues eastward along the Harbour Road but turns up and inland to meet the Stanley 'bypass' road. It may be difficult to guess who would by-pass Stanley when it holds more than 2,100 of the islands' 2,900 residents, but

WHILE YOU'RE THERE

While in Stanley, the capital of the Falkland Islands, immerse yourself in history by visiting local attractions such as the **Falkland Islands Museum**, the **Government House**, and the **Anglican Christ Church Cathedral**. Other interesting landmarks to admire are a whalebone arch, a totem pole, and several war memorials and shipwrecks in the harbor. The Falklands are a prime **penguin-watching** location, and day tours are available out of Stanley to places where you can stand stock-still and have three different species of penguin waddling by within a metre and completely unconcerned by your presence. Grab a bite at the renowned **Woodbine Café** fish and chip shop, which just last year celebrated its 30th anniversary on the island.

RACE DETAILS

WHEN? Mid March

WHEN TO APPLY: If registration is submitted before February 26, runners receive a discount on their entry fee.

HOW MANY TAKE PART? 75

DIFFICULTY RATING: 8/10

SPECIAL CONSIDERATIONS: Race instructions alert to the possibility of inclement weather and inevitable summer winds. It is unlikely that any environmental condition will cancel the race but, if bad enough, the start may be briefly delayed. Do not forget your sunscreen and head coverings, for 'The Hole in the Ozone Layer' lies above you.

CONTACT:
Standard Chartered Bank
PO Box 597, Ross Road
Stanley FIQQ 1ZZ
Falkland Islands
☎ 500 22220
✉ bank.info@sc.com
💻 www.sc.com/fk/marathon

the road leads slightly downhill to the old Stanley Airport built by Argentina in 1972. Since the new military airport was built some distance to the west after the conflict you can now only get planes from here to elsewhere in the islands or to Antarctica.

But runners make a turn in the airport car park and head back along the bypass road for about 9km (5½ miles). It climbs, dips and then climbs again to reach the westerly turning point on Sapper Hill, just before the asphalt road runs out. In the first few years the race was run, the land around here was still littered with landmines left over from the war. Mine clearance had been halted due to casualties but re-started in 2009, and Sapper Hill Corral was declared free of mines in 2012.

Runners repeat the run back down to the old airport before taking the third turn which points them back towards town. Even then it's not quite enough road that's been covered, so runners have to repeat the loop out to Beaver Hangar again.

As an out-and-back course, you won't be able to avoid the wind gusting into your face at some point. Sunscreen and head covering are important despite the often cold weather: this is the location of the 'Hole in the Ozone Layer'.

To reach the islands is a marathon feat in itself. One woman flew all the way from Hong Kong, taking four days to do so, and only arriving 20 hours before the start because of the restrictive once-a-week commercial flight schedule.

At the last count there were 75 marathon runners (63 men, 12 women) and 22 relay teams, as well as 54 entries in the 3km (2 mile) Fun Run. The race supports the global charity of Standard Chartered Bank, 'Seeing is Believing', and the entire bank staff turn out as volunteers on race day. The course record of 2:35:39 by a local schoolteacher is impressive in the circumstances.

While being far from your usual marathon experience, Stanley is definitely one to have under your belt as you look back on your marathon ventures. With the regularly small numbers of entrants, you will be part of the 1 in 12 million of the world's population to have ever run on these roads.

Previous page: The Falklands War Memorial is a landmark in the first mile of the race.

Left: A commemorative totem pole has been created on the Stanley Airport Road showing that all roads lead north, away from nearby Antarctica.

Run Barbados Marathon | Barbados

'Come for the run, stay for the fun' is the invitation from Barbados Tourism & Marketing Inc. The Barbados Race Series has hosted many a serious athlete, including olympic medalists, since it started in 1983.

The sun is what draws visitors to the island, but when it comes to the race all efforts are in place to avoid it. The marathon starts at 4.30am, it gets light at 5.40am, and less than an hour later it already feels hot. Even though midday temperatures are not often greater than 30°C (86°F), the direct sun beating down takes its toll.

'Run Barbados' has been through many different configurations over the 32 years of its existence. In recent years it got somewhat stuck in the doldrums and dropped the marathon in favour of the shorter events (1 mile, 5km, 10km and half marathon). The latest edition reinstated it. New specialist organisers were brought in and the event appears poised for a re-birth.

The race starts on the Bay Street Esplanade just outside the Prime Minister's office on the south side of Bridgetown. Running in the pre-dawn darkness through the empty shuttered streets of Bridgetown has a slightly eerie feel. Even when you have passed the harbour and are heading north on the Spring Garden Highway alongside the beach at 5km (3 miles), the only audible sounds are the breathing and footfall of fellow runners (unless, that is, you are close enough to the front to hear the pounding bass of the speakers on the support vehicle accompanying the leaders). The course clings closely to the shoreline, so remains level in the main. After 6km (3¾ miles) at the Esso refinery it diverts inland a little up an incline before reverting to the shoreline, backing palm-fringed, white sand beaches. The sense of detachment only lessens after reaching the residential areas, where women in nightgowns, up early to get Sunday lunch on the go before attending church, appear in front gardens to pass comment and cups of water where needed. The views are varied – sometimes out to sea across a slither of white sand, and sometimes past roadside shops

41

WHILE YOU'RE THERE

If you can ever be tired of the beach and want to do something different, **Farley Hill National Park** consists of acres of tropical trees and plants set on a cliff 75m (250ft) above the sea. It overlooks the entire Scotland District. No visit is complete without a visit to a rum distillery. **Mount Gay** offers one of the finest, and gives tours of its distillery. See: www.barbados.org.

Above right: Less than 100 people run the marathon course, so plenty of motivation is required to keep going on what might seem a lonely road.

Right: The marathon event takes in a range of other races for fun runners, including a 5km run, a 10km run, and half marathon wheelchair events.

and houses with banana palms, breadfruit trees, bougainvillea and vividly variegated croton hedges busting out from every spare bit of earth. After the tiny fish market in Paynes Bay both marathon and half marathon runners make the turn to head back towards Bridgetown.

All Run Barbados courses wind through the streets of this historic and well-preserved seaport that dates back to the seventeenth century. With dawn having broken, runners can appreciate picturesque views of the Careenage, Parliament Buildings, Independence Square, and Lord Nelson's Statue (smaller but older than its more famous equivalent in London).

Runners cross Independence Bridge and hit Bay Street, which traces the sweeping curve of Bridgetown's Carlisle Bay. After crossing the finish line, half marathon runners can walk around the back of the bandstand and into those inviting waters. For marathon runners it's a pleasure postponed until they have completed their second lap.

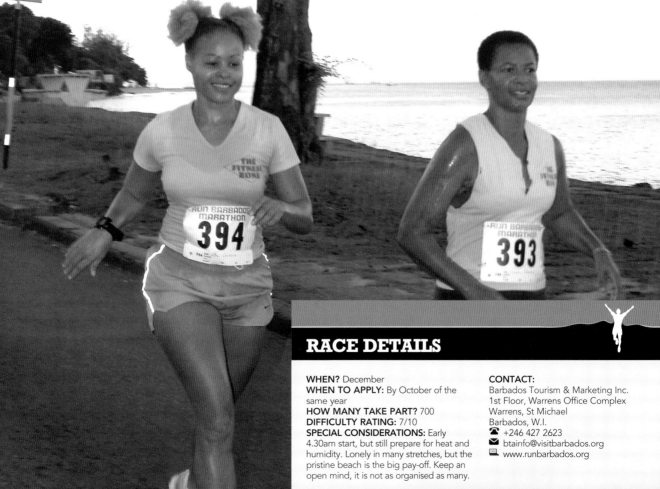

RACE DETAILS

WHEN? December
WHEN TO APPLY: By October of the same year
HOW MANY TAKE PART? 700
DIFFICULTY RATING: 7/10
SPECIAL CONSIDERATIONS: Early 4.30am start, but still prepare for heat and humidity. Lonely in many stretches, but the pristine beach is the big pay-off. Keep an open mind, it is not as organised as many.

CONTACT:
Barbados Tourism & Marketing Inc.
1st Floor, Warrens Office Complex
Warrens, St Michael
Barbados, W.I.
☎ +246 427 2623
✉ btainfo@visitbarbados.org
🖳 www.runbarbados.org

Volcano Marathon | Chile

42

WHILE YOU'RE THERE

Your Volcano Marathon registration fee includes a 5-day stay in San Pedro de Atacama, including planned excursions to the **Salt Mountain Range**, **Valley of the Moon**, and **Valley of Death**. These trips into the desert illuminate massive stone and sand formations that have been carved through thousands of years of wind and water erosion. The **Meteorite Museum** is another out-of-this-world experience in the lunar landscape of San Pedro. The **R.P. Gustavo Le Paige Archeological Museum**, although no longer host to the exceptionally well-preserved mummies for which the town is famous, is still worth several hours of close attention. The biggest opencast copper mine in the world is located 100km (62 miles) away at **Chuquicamata**. Just to stand at a roadside location overlooking the huge excavation is enough to provide an experience you will remember.

The first challenge for entrants to the Volcano Marathon is to get themselves to the startline. The race advice tersely states: 'Competitors assemble at San Pedro de Atacama'.

But wait – 'Atacama' – isn't that the desert that I learned in school was the driest place on Earth? Yes it is - as the organisers explain: '…in the heart of the Atacama Desert, the driest desert in the world'.

Quite unrelated to running, I visited this then dusty village in 1973 when travelling overland in South America because it was famous for the well-preserved mummies on display in the local church. The Gustavo Le Paige Archaeological Museum now features artefacts from the first inhabitants of the area – but the mummies are no longer displayed. The roads are now paved, but the nearest airport is in Calama, 100km (62 miles)

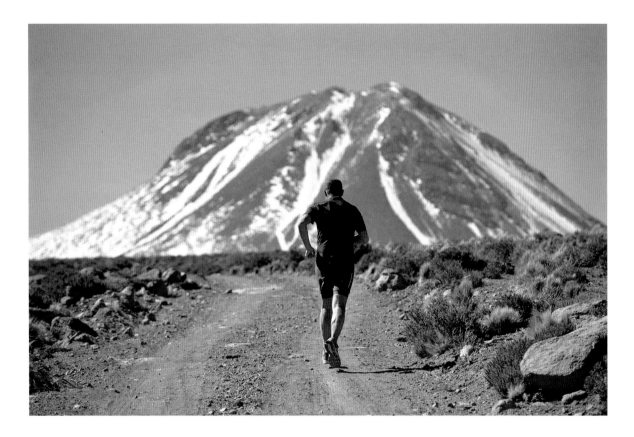

away, and offers only domestic flights. The Chilean capital, Santiago, lies several hundred kilometres to the south, with several buses a day plying the route. The race entry fee of 3,000 euros includes five days' accommodation in a luxury San Pedro hotel. That length of time is needed both to recover from the journey and to minimally acclimatise to the 2,600m (8,530ft) altitude. Local excursions are put on to such evocatively named places as the Salt Mountain Range, the Valley of the Moon and the Valley of Death.

Acclimatisation can only be minimal because the race starts at 4,475m (14,700ft) near the Tropic of Capricorn and adjacent to the Lascar Volcano, one of the most active volcanoes in northern Chile. The impact of thinner air is ameliorated by the course being overall downhill, but the spectacular panoramic views of up to 10 volcanoes also takes the breath away.

The first half of the race is on dirt roads at an average of over 4,000m (13,123ft) altitude. There are manned aid stations at 10km (6 miles) and at halfway. At the third checkpoint at 30km (19 miles) the course ascends 2km (1 mile) off-road. From 35km (22 miles) runners face rough terrain alongside a gorge for the next 5km (3 miles). The finish

Left: It's a long journey to reach this race site in Chile, with the nearest airport 100km (62 miles) away, but the breathtaking scenery and one-of-a-kind challenge makes it worth it.

Above: Runners must arrive a few days early to acclimate to the high altitude of the region, where they will be racing among mountains – and, of course, a volcano.

line lies at 3,600m (11,800ft) where the temperature could be up to 30°C (86°F).

The Volcano Marathon is more than just a race. The pre-race visits are to places that appear other-worldly. The surreal, lunar shapes of Valley of the Moon (Valle de la Luna) are bathed in striking colours of red, pink and gold at sunset. The Valley of Death (Valle de la Muerte) features gigantic sand dunes and rocks that resemble the surface of Mars so much so that it is where NASA tests equipment when planning missions to the Red Planet.

Below: Japanese competitor, Yusuke Mamada, tackles a sand dune in the Valley of Death.

Right: Dutch participant Taco Jongman celebrates on reaching the finish line after traversing the driest desert in the world.

RACE DETAILS

WHEN? Mid November
WHEN TO APPLY: As early as possible, first come first served basis
HOW MANY TAKE PART? 40
DIFFICULTY RATING: 10/10
SPECIAL CONSIDERATIONS: The Volcano Marathon necessitates extra preparation for distance running at high altitude and in high desert heat. Participation in the marathon requires runners to arrive at least 3 days prior to the race to acclimate to the reduced oxygen levels of the area.

CONTACT:
Richard Donovan, Race Director
Polar Running Adventures
95 Rosan Glas
Rahoon Road, Galway
Ireland
☎ 353 91 51 6644
✉ npmarathon@gmail.com
▭ www.volcanomarathon.com

Boston Marathon | USA

The Boston Marathon is the oldest annual marathon in the world, having been run continuously since 1897, the year after the first Modern Olympics of 1896, for which the modern marathon was invented. Back then there were just 18 people running. During the centenary edition in 1996 more than 35,000 people ran. The 1996 marathon was the first to see such a high number of runners. In that year people did not have to run a qualifying time to be accepted. Usually, in order to qualify, every runner must have finished a certified marathon within a specified (fast) time dependent on the age of the runner. The qualifying standard is high enough to make qualifying for Boston – also known as 'to BQ' – an achievement in itself.

The Boston Marathon for many years fell short of the marathon distance. In 1907, the start was moved west from Ashland to Hopkinton, but the distance remained no more than 39km (24½ miles) until 1924, and even between 1951 and 1956 it was only 40.5km (25 miles). The route travels east and gently downhill for the first half, but then drops more sharply until reaching the famous four Newton Hills, among which lies so-called 'heartbreak hill'. This hill does not, as one may think, get its name from runners heartbroken because they have to conquer yet another ascent, but the name does originate in the Boston Marathon. The story relates that during the 1936 race defending champion, John A. Kelley, caught up with race leader, Ellison 'Tarzan' Brown, giving him a consolatory pat on the shoulder as he overtook him. This overbearing gesture apparently riled Tarzan sufficiently and he went on to retake the lead and win the race. In the words of a local journalist, the bitter defeat 'broke Kelley's heart'.

From here, the course again gently descends to the finish in the centre of Boston. Overall the course drops 135m (440ft) from start to finish, or 3.3m (10¾ft) for every 1km (¾ mile) of its length. This gravitational advantage for runners is

WHILE YOU'RE THERE

Home to one of the new world's most famous universities, **Harvard sits just across the river** from the marathon area, and is well worth a visit. The area is not just an academic hotbed but a brilliant place for finding independent record shops. **Newbury Street** offers some of the finest boutique shopping in the US. Stay on the cerebral path with a visit to the **JFK Library**, then chow down on Boston's famous lobster roll at the **James Hook** eatery. See: www.bostonusa.com

Right: The Boston Marathon is run on Patriot Day on 11 September.

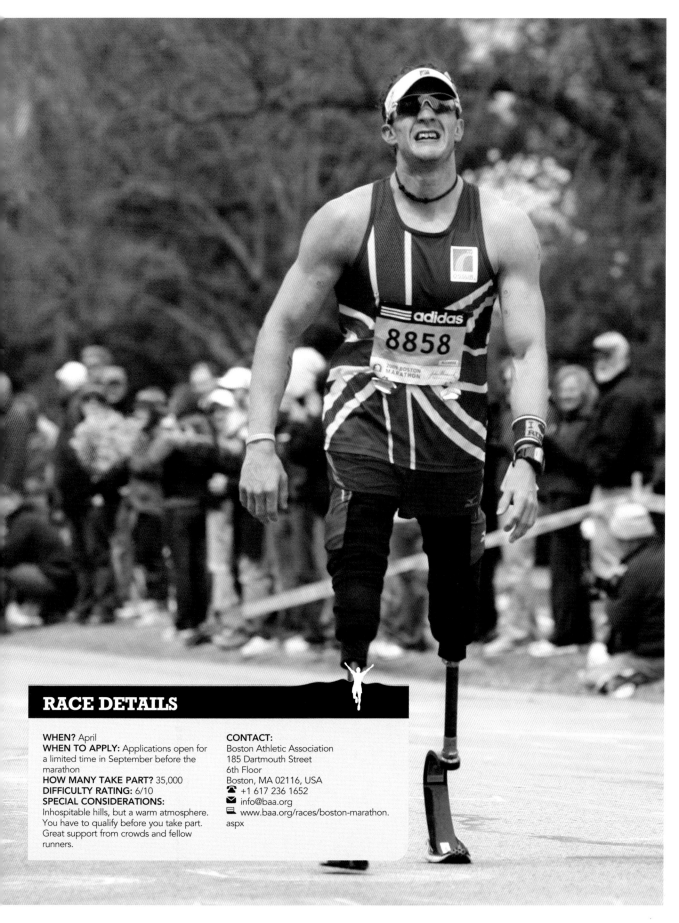

RACE DETAILS

WHEN? April
WHEN TO APPLY: Applications open for a limited time in September before the marathon
HOW MANY TAKE PART? 35,000
DIFFICULTY RATING: 6/10
SPECIAL CONSIDERATIONS:
Inhospitable hills, but a warm atmosphere. You have to qualify before you take part. Great support from crowds and fellow runners.

CONTACT:
Boston Athletic Association
185 Dartmouth Street
6th Floor
Boston, MA 02116, USA
☎ +1 617 236 1652
✉ info@baa.org
🖥 www.baa.org/races/boston-marathon. aspx

on occasions supplemented by an assisting wind. Such was the case in 1994 when Cosmas Ndeti won and again in 2011, when a strong tailwind helped to push Geoffrey Mutai to what was then the fastest time ever run over the marathon distance, at 2:03:02. The time cannot be recognised as a record (in fact, no times recorded in Boston can) because of the advantages afforded by overall gradient and wind direction.

In most years Boston has not produced particularly fast times, perhaps partly because the general rhythm of running downhill for the first 25km (15½ miles) is disturbed by the following uphill section. At other times, the adversity of the conditions, varying from freezing rain to boiling heat, are a factor that can affect times significantly. What the race has produced are a number of thrillingly competitive duels, such as Bill Rodgers against Jeff Wells in 1978, and Alberto Salazar against Dick Beardsley in 1982. In recent years, it has been the elite women, who start separately before the mass race, who have given Boston's avid marathon aficionados the most dramatic denouements.

Below: Everyone who runs the Boston Marathon has to qualify by running another marathon in a fast time.

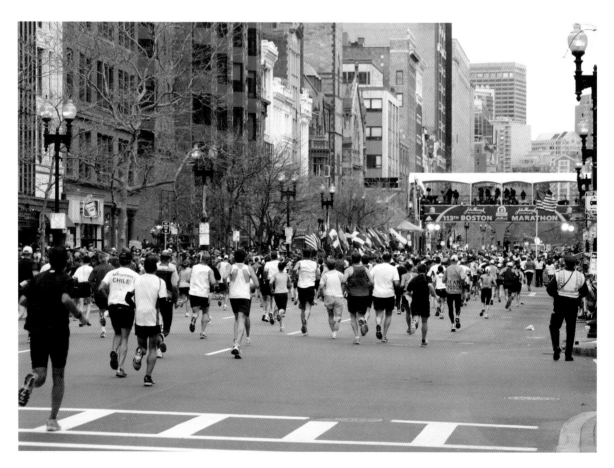

TCS New York City Marathon | USA

Just like anything in the Big Apple, this race is on a monumental scale; it is the biggest marathon there is, with upwards of 50,000 runners taking part.

New York staged the first marathon in the Western Hemisphere in September 1896, soon after the Athens Olympics but, unlike the Boston race which was held six months later, it did not survive. New York re-established a marathon in 1970. Fred Lebow, originally from Romanian Transylvania, worked in the New York rag trade when he organised a marathon of four laps entirely within Central Park. It was a low-key affair with each runner paying a modest US $1 entry fee. Just 55 of the 127 entrants finished the race.

It was not until the 1976 race, which coincided with the American Bicentennial, that things took off and the New York Marathon was re-invented as the model for all other mass marathons. It started with a suggestion from Ted Corbitt, a well-known local runner, to invite teams from the five boroughs of the city to compete in the race. Somehow, City Hall interpreted this as a city-wide race through the five boroughs – and they jumped on the idea. Lebow was against this at first, seeing the logistical problems more clearly than the city mandarins.

WHILE YOU'RE THERE

In New York City, the options on tours are seemingly limitless. Take a **pizza tour of Brooklyn**; a tour of **gangster sites in New York**; a **tour of film locations**; a **hip hop tour of Harlem**; even a rather gruesome tour of where famous people have died. There are also plenty of transport options – walking, biking, metro or the ubiquitous yellow taxi. For post-marathon hunger pangs, one of the favourite spots for locals is **Shake Shack** with many locations across NYC, including a new one in Battery Park City. See: www.nycgo.com

Left: The New York City Marathon has a competitive field for wheelchair races.

A new route transformed the old race and introduced a new start point on Staten Island at the iconic Verazzano Bridge. No longer confined within Central Park, people could not help but pay attention when the marathon went through main-city thoroughfares. People relished the chance to run in such a public spectacle and entries poured in until the 2,100 cap set that year was reached. In subsequent years the entries rapidly escalated, reaching 14,000 by 1979.

The course offers a sightseeing tour as well as a sporting event, travelling through parts of the city that many tourists would never see. It offers awe-inspiring views of New York Harbour, the Statue of Liberty and Lower Manhattan, as well as a tough, but exhilarating, climb over 59th Street Bridge. On reaching Manhattan, runners take a long northward turn up First Avenue to the Bronx, before doubling back to the Central Park finish by way of Harlem and Fifth Avenue.

Most events, dwarfed by the sheer size of the city, struggle to capture the imagination of the average New Yorker.

Above: Many runners report that this marathon is an unforgettable experience, with flawless organisation and energetic public support.

RACE DETAILS

WHEN? November
WHEN TO APPLY: November of the year before
HOW MANY TAKE PART? 45,000
DIFFICULTY RATING: 6/10
SPECIAL CONSIDERATIONS: Early morning start in November means the weather can be very chilly, so pack the thermals. Lots of inclines and bridges, as well as masses of people, it can get crowded, especially at the start. Leave plenty of time to get there.

CONTACT:
ING New York City Marathon
New York Road Runners
322 Columbus Avenue
New York, NY 10023, USA
☎ +1 855 569 6977
✉ help.tcsnycmarathon.org
🖳 www.ingnycmarathon.org

Above: Moral support is provided all the way around this course.

Marathon day is different. On the first Sunday of November New Yorkers stop what they are doing and come out to cheer on the runners. More than 100 live bands play along the course turning the event into a mini-carnival.

Each year 100,000 people apply to take one of the 50,000 places on offer. Organisers charge a hefty premium to overseas tour operators for allotted places, knowing that the appeal of this run can readily prise open runners' purses.

In 1976, the organisers of the New York Marathon created a template for every modern marathon. The race was no longer just about finding a loop in which to cover the required distance, it became a way to unite a city, allowing participants to take a grand tour of New York and experience something truly magical. This spirit lives on in the modern race and has ignited a passion for marathon running that has spread around the globe. Much as a debt is owed to the original Athens Marathon, so too must the vision of the New York Marathon organisers be appreciated by every marathon enthusiast.

Marine Corps Marathon | USA

The Marine Corps Marathon styles itself as 'The People's Race', relying on the appreciation of ordinary runners rather than trying to entice an elite field – unusually there is no prize money on offer. Since the 9/11 tragedy in 2001, running this most patriotic of American marathons has often been undertaken as a mark of respect to those who have been victims of war, whether civilians or those in the armed forces.

Of the 30,000 participants who enter each year – and places are usually snapped up within a few hours of the online entry opening – an average of 40 per cent are attempting their first marathon. The race is for the glory of running itself, with participants drawn by the smooth, flat surface of the course, and the chance to tour the US capital.

WHILE YOU'RE THERE

The Marine Corps Marathon takes place in the capital. While it might not have the buzz of New York, it is overflowing with famous landmarks, such as **The White House**, **Capitol Hill**, and the **Lincoln Memorial**. Abraham Lincoln is probably one president you'll want to see while in the city – his monument is more like a temple, adorned with 36 Doric columns, and is at the heart of the main attractions. Washington is also home to the **Smithsonian**, the world's largest museum complex.

Left: The Marine Corps Marathon is a race that embodies pure, unashamed patriotism.

Right: The landmarks are just one part of the appeal of this marathon: many US citizens run it as a way to publicly support the work of the US troops.

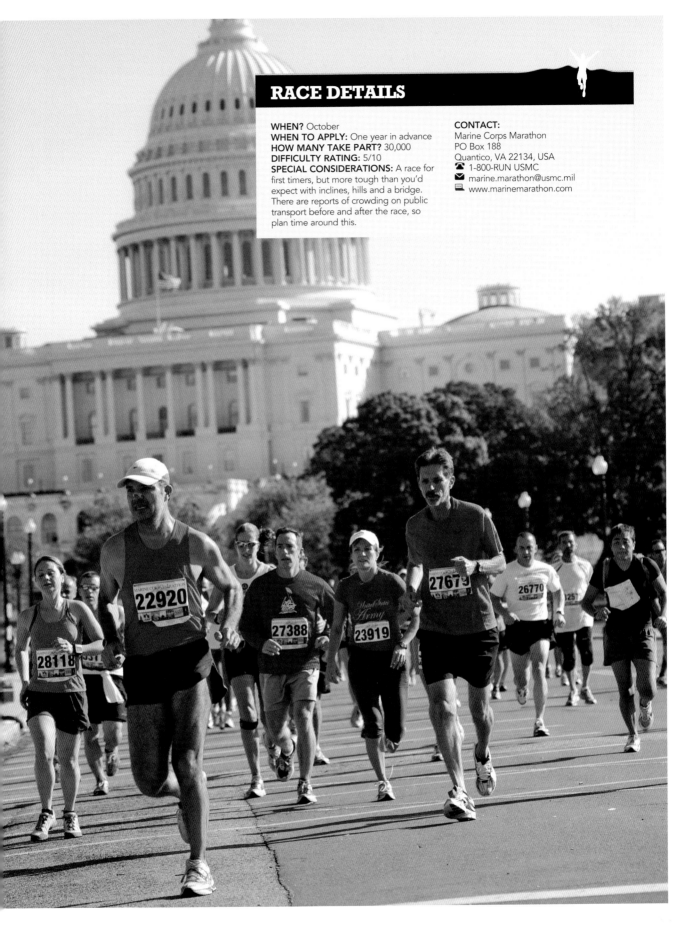

RACE DETAILS

WHEN? October
WHEN TO APPLY: One year in advance
HOW MANY TAKE PART? 30,000
DIFFICULTY RATING: 5/10
SPECIAL CONSIDERATIONS: A race for first timers, but more tough than you'd expect with inclines, hills and a bridge. There are reports of crowding on public transport before and after the race, so plan time around this.

CONTACT:
Marine Corps Marathon
PO Box 188
Quantico, VA 22134, USA
☎ 1-800-RUN USMC
✉ marine.marathon@usmc.mil
🖥 www.marinemarathon.com

The race starts with the national anthem, pledging allegiance to the flag, and a flurry of star-spangled banners waving in the autumnal light. It is an inclusive sort of patriotism, as plenty of non-US runners are among the crowd, waving flags from their home nations. A supersonic flyover of F/A-18 Hornet attack fighter jets and CH-53 Sea Stallion helicopters make a suitably dramatic opening to this great race.

The course meanders around the lower reaches of the Potomac River, with the topographical high points coming at 5km (3 miles) and 13km (8 miles), but all the major sights are saved for much later in the race at 25–32km (15½–20 miles). At this point, runners circumnavigate the Reflecting Pool, pass by the Lincoln Memorial, then along Constitution Avenue with the White House and the Washington Memorial to each side, followed by the museums, the Grant Memorial and finally the Capitol. After this touristic tour de force, runners cross back over the Potomac for the final few kilometres, passing the Pentagon and reaching the Iwo Jima Memorial at the finish line.

Even without considering the monuments, the city appears at its best at the time of the race, with trees in vivid autumnal colors.

Above: The race provides the occasion to revel in the military pride of the US and the service given by the country's combat forces, their friends and families.

Reggae Marathon | Jamaica

The Reggae marathon is a carnival, a food festival and a music extravaganza all in one. Organisers aim to attract runners from all over the world to sample what they call 'running in paradise'. This world event started on a local footing with a loose collection of runners gathering at Kingston's reservoir, nicknamed 'The Dam'. They formed a club called the 'Jamdammers' in 1995 and to celebrate their fifth birthday the Reggae Marathon was born. Now into its second decade, the Reggae Marathon has its own unique character.

The race name is not surprising considering Jamaica was the birthplace of Reggae music legend Bob Marley. Such is his legacy that Marley's sons have run this race, but the course is as much as an attraction as the music. The Reggae Marathon takes place on the first Saturday in December and starts in the dark at 5.15am when it is what the locals call 'chilly', but which those from cooler climes might consider as balmy. Chilly, in the context of a Jamaican winter, means about 25°C (77°F). When the sun gets up (just a couple of hours after the start of the race) the temperature rises to 32°C (90°F).

Below: The local people turn out in force to support the runners of this appealing marathon.

Preceding the marathon is what's billed as the best pasta party in the world, with plenty of dishes with a distinct, local flavour. On race day itself, a flaming tiki (bamboo) torch procession lends an almost mystical quality to the scene as runners gather at the start line, which is enhanced by the unmistakable Caribbean sound of Rasta drummers. Runners head south along Long Bay to the Negril Roundabout, where they then turn back to return to the start.

The 10km runners stop here, but the half-marathon runners go on to a second turning point at the other end of Long Bay before returning. Marathon runners go further along the scenic coast road, with beaches to the left and marshland called the 'Great Morass' to the right. Several of the place names here – Bloody Bay and Crocodile Rock, for example – sound as if they have come directly from a pirate captain's treasure map.

WHILE YOU'RE THERE

Jamaica may seem like it is packed with tourists, but there are still many hidden gems to explore. The beaches are a given, among the most loved by locals is **Dr's Cave**. The **Blue Mountains** are best known for coffee and good for hiking, and wildlife trails. There is also **Golden Eye**, the home of Bond writer Ian Fleming, with the island often used as a location for 007 films. See: www. visitjamaica.com.

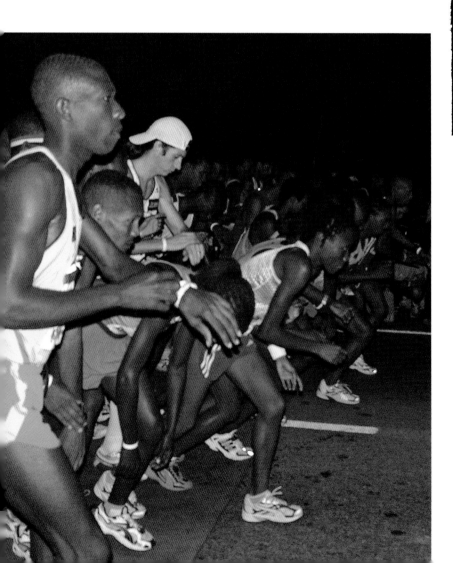

Left: The races in this series start at Long Bay Beach Resort, halfway along the 11km (7 mile) white sand beach. It's an early start for the competitors to make the best of the cool morning.

Below: The leaders in the field will be home and finished before the day has started for most people.

Along with the impressive natural scenery comes the manmade enhancements of sound systems, DJ booths, and cars with speakers strapped to the roof, pumping out bass. The wayside crowds are also on hand to lend their support. This can vary from spraying water, handing out bottles of glucose drinks, or blasting out their own reggae classics to keep the rhythm alive.

Barbecue smoke wafts from the finishing line as the race seamlessly moves into one big after-party, featuring the latest reggae acts and a full Jamaican menu of jerk chicken and curry goat with rice and peas. A post-marathon breakfast is offered in the appropriately named town of Margaritaville. Just make sure you cross the finish line before you go there.

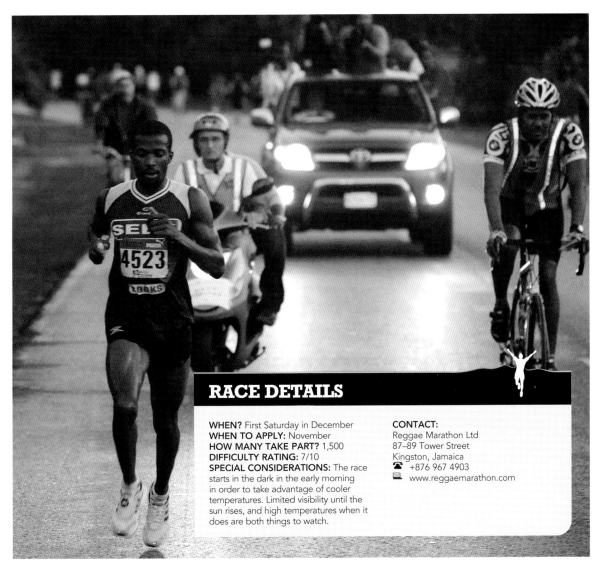

RACE DETAILS

WHEN? First Saturday in December
WHEN TO APPLY: November
HOW MANY TAKE PART? 1,500
DIFFICULTY RATING: 7/10
SPECIAL CONSIDERATIONS: The race starts in the dark in the early morning in order to take advantage of cooler temperatures. Limited visibility until the sun rises, and high temperatures when it does are both things to watch.

CONTACT:
Reggae Marathon Ltd
87–89 Tower Street
Kingston, Jamaica
☎ +876 967 4903
🖥 www.reggaemarathon.com

Toronto Waterfront
Marathon | Canada

With three of the biggest marathon courses in North America – New York, Boston and Chicago – on its doorstep, Toronto might well have been forgiven if it had hosted a lesser event. But this marathon, like those of other major cities, confidently attracts elite runners to its international-standard course.

The reason is Lake Ontario. There is an undeniable something about running beside the water, and Toronto took that idea and ran with it. All 42.2km (26 miles 385 yards) that make up the course of the Scotiabank Toronto Waterfront Marathon overlook the water.

Toronto has another card to play. Surprising as it may seem, the United Nations declares the Canadian metropolis to be the most ethnically diverse city in the world, with almost half of its population coming from outside Canada's borders. Runners from all parts of the world can feel at home here. Nationalities that would declare themselves sworn enemies in other parts of the world seem to find common cause in Toronto. The race celebrates such diversity by deliberately steering a course through 10 different ethnic districts, each with their own style of celebrating the marathon. Runners go through Little Poland, Little Italy and toward the Caribbean, and then encounter the colourful costumes of Little India. Bollywood-beats then set the racing rhythm onward to Little Asia, where 16 bands play, successfully elevating the running spirit.

This race started life as a half marathon in 1990 and after some success was extended to full marathon. The signature waterfront course was adopted in 1999 and, with its wide, scenic route, paved the way for future expansion. Adroit marketing of the marathon as a more accessible alternative to New York, targeted primarily at the British and then the Mexican marathon markets paid off, and foreign participation in the race began to emulate the diversity of the local population.

WHILE YOU'RE THERE

The city is often noted for its skyline, but the best way to see it is from across the water. **Toronto Islands** are a quick ferry ride away and the view of the city is stunning. There is an amusement park here, as well as gardens, walking trails and a beach. It is the place the locals go to escape. If you want street life, explore the many ethnic neighbourhoods of the inner city, including the aromatic **Chinatown**. **Little Tokyo** offers some of the best sushi on the planet. Crime has recently become a problem in some areas of the city, so double check with your hotel where is safe. See: www.seetoronto.now

Above right: The CN Tower is a notable landmark that is clearly visible in this Toronto Waterfront Marathon.

Right: The balloon arches indicate that the finish line is not too far away.

In terms of performance, a Guinness World Record for 'joggling' – the fringe sport of jogging and juggling at the same time – was set by 'The Joggler' when he ran a course of 3 hours and 7 minutes in 2005. And 73-year-old local Ed Whitlock established a truly astonishing world age-best of 2:54. In recent years the open age group has emulated Whitlock's effort, with the course record rapidly improving from 2:09 to 2:08 and now 2:07. Whitlock himself set an over-80 world best of 3:15:54 in the 2011 race.

Both the marathon and half marathon start from the same spot in downtown Toronto. After 18km (11 miles), half-marathon runners branch off to the finish while the marathon runners head on to make a tour of the eastern side of town. Peer across the water and you'll see the city skyline, and one of the tallest buildings in the world, the CN Tower, before heading forward to the beaches district and then on to the finish.

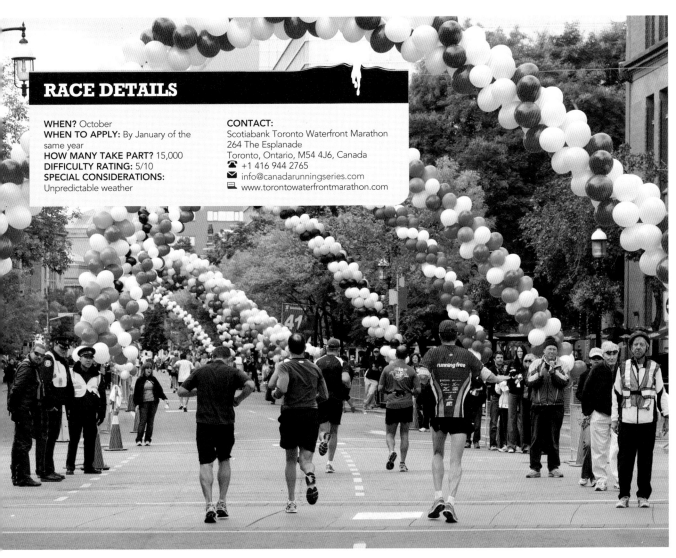

RACE DETAILS

WHEN? October
WHEN TO APPLY: By January of the same year
HOW MANY TAKE PART? 15,000
DIFFICULTY RATING: 5/10
SPECIAL CONSIDERATIONS: Unpredictable weather

CONTACT:
Scotiabank Toronto Waterfront Marathon
264 The Esplanade
Toronto, Ontario, M54 4J6, Canada
☎ +1 416 944 2765
✉ info@canadarunningseries.com
🖥 www.torontowaterfrontmarathon.com

Niagara Falls International Marathon
USA & Canada

Few marathons start in one country and finish in another, but that is only half the claim to fame of the Niagara Falls International Marathon. The other half is the location of the finish line – within drifting distance of the spray arising from the Falls themselves.

The idea for a marathon from Buffalo, New York, USA, to Niagara Falls, Ontario, Canada, was conceived by a handful of musician runners from the Buffalo Philharmonic who regularly did a long run from the Peace Bridge in Fort Erie to the Rainbow Bridge in Niagara Falls, a distance of 30km (18½ miles).

They called the run 'bridge to bridge', recalls Jesse Kregal, a timpanist who was part of the original group. Families would go along and meet the runners at the end for a picnic.

WHILE YOU'RE THERE
Niagara Falls actually refers to three waterfalls in the area, all worth close inspection. They include the **Canadian Horseshoe Falls**, **Bridal Veil Falls** and the **American Falls**. Niagara is a city of 82,500, but every year the Falls attract more than 14 million visitors from around the world so it bursts with a cosmopolitan flavour. There are two casinos, three water parks and a selection of dinner theatres. Just 30km (18½ miles) north, where the Niagara flows into Lake Ontario, is the Town of **Niagara-on-the-Lake**, one of Canada's most beautiful communities and home to the famous **Shaw Festival Theatre**.

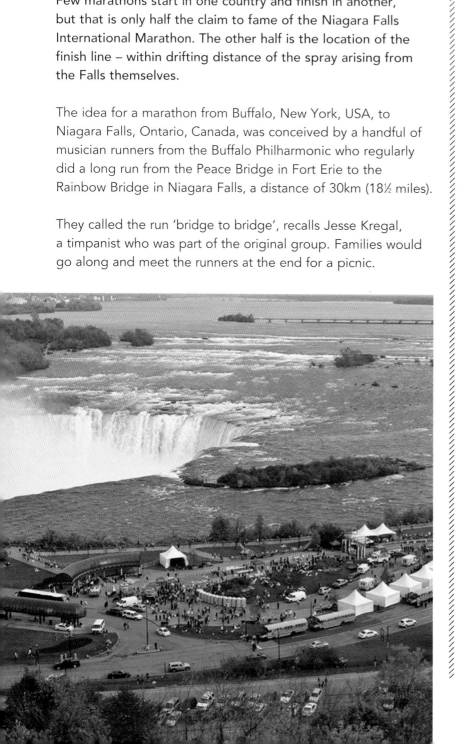

Left: This is a flat and fast course with plenty of organised on-course support.

Right: For most runners the scenic route and awe-inspiring finish are what makes this marathon magical.

Over page: The season is evident throughout this course, with the varied colours of the foliage.

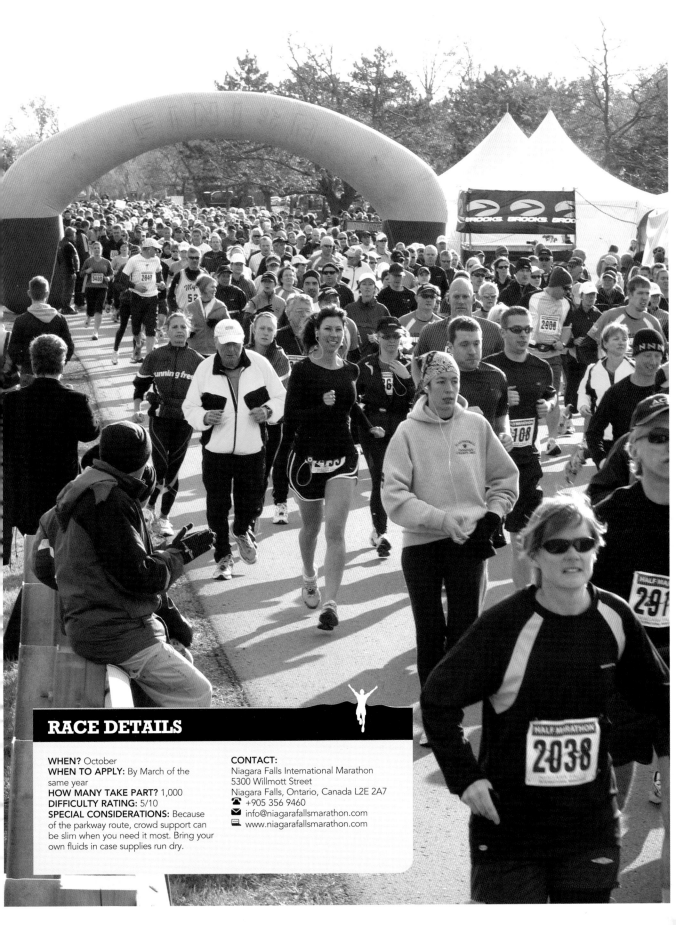

RACE DETAILS

WHEN? October
WHEN TO APPLY: By March of the same year
HOW MANY TAKE PART? 1,000
DIFFICULTY RATING: 5/10
SPECIAL CONSIDERATIONS: Because of the parkway route, crowd support can be slim when you need it most. Bring your own fluids in case supplies run dry.

CONTACT:
Niagara Falls International Marathon
5300 Willmott Street
Niagara Falls, Ontario, Canada L2E 2A7
☎ +905 356 9460
✉ info@niagarafallsmarathon.com
🖥 www.niagarafallsmarathon.com

'Then we had the bright idea of having a race that would start some place in Buffalo and end at the Falls,' said Kregal, a one-time race director. Runners gear up for the race in the unusual surroundings of an art gallery. The start of the race in Buffalo is low-key, as runners practically slink out of town to cross the Peace Bridge into Canada. There is a light sprinkling of support along the route, mainly from local people, but the main reward comes from the stunning natural scenery.

The idea of 1,000 runners streaming unchecked across the border at first seemed an insurmountable problem, but Canadian immigration was persuaded to pre-check and approve participants' passports. That done, the inaugural marathon was held on 26 October 1974, and the race has continued to attract runners in their thousands. This is largely due to the autumnal beauty of the scenery along roads that Winston Churchill called 'the most stunning Sunday drive in the world.'

For others, the highlight of the race comes early, as they cross from the USA into Canada after about 8km (5 miles). To the left is the vast expanse of Lake Erie, and to the right is the beginning of the Niagara River Parkway. In clear weather it is possible to see the plume of white mist rising from the Falls, 27km (16¾ miles) downriver. The finish lies just 50m (164ft) from the Canadian Horseshoe Falls, a natural wonder that draws 14-million visitors a year.

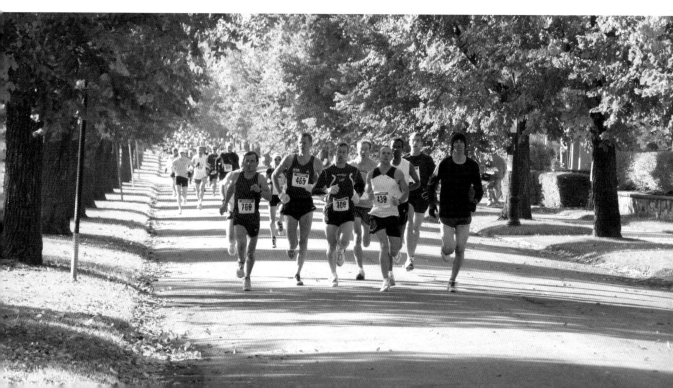

Havana Marathon | Cuba

Like most of what is on show in the Cuban capital, the 'Marabana' event may not be able to rival the bigger international marathons, but it offers an intimate glimpse into the character of the place. You will feel privileged to run alongside locals who make do without all the technological trappings that runners seem to find necessary elsewhere.

Going without energy gels or power drinks, and technological textiles that 'wick' your sweat away is quite usual here, so if you can't do without them, then bring your own. It is much as marathons used to be before the marketing people got to work, except that some people do not have running shoes either. In response, many regular runners from overseas bring a pair of old running shoes to donate to their unshod fellow competitors in a true spirit of camaraderie.

The event may appear random and spontaneous, with even the registration process being put together just hours before the starting gun is fired. Often there's an Olympic champion, such as Alberto Juantorena, Ana Quirot or Javier Sotomayor, to wave the flag that begins the race.

WHILE YOU'RE THERE

You can read all about the history of Cuba at the **Museo de la Revolución** where the revolutionary ideals are set out and the story of the modern state is recorded. There is a loving shrine to **Che Guevara**, including locks of his hair and fragments of his socks. You cannot leave without taking a **tour of the city** in a '50s Cadillac – kept in working order. Stop at the **cigar factory** too, to see how the country's world famous cigars are made.

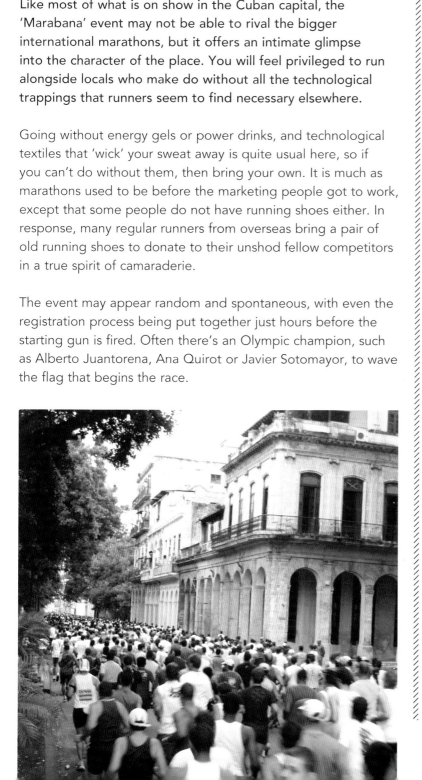

Left: The Havana Marathon consists of two laps of a city that has an old world charm.

The course is two laps, and a half marathon is run at the same time over a single lap. Starting at Paseo del Prado, the run heads down towards the Malecón, a broad boulevard onto which Atlantic breakers crash, dashing spray over the roadway and runners alike. The route goes inland to the Raúl Diaz Sports Complex before turning back towards Habana Old Town, El Capitolio and the Malecón, passing by the monumental public space and statuary of the Plaza de la Revolución along the way.

Conditions can be hot and humid, but there are water and orange stations every 2–3km (1½ miles). Havana is a mildly testing event topographically, but more challenging and infinitely more rewarding in cultural terms. The first 9km (5½ miles) along the coast is flat before you turn inland, then the course becomes hilly for the remainder of the lap. On those grounds, it is all the more suitable for beginners keen for a running adventure.

Above: Havana is a UNESCO World Heritage city and the marathon route takes full advantage of all it has to offer.

Right: The course of the marathon is not made exclusive to marathon runners.

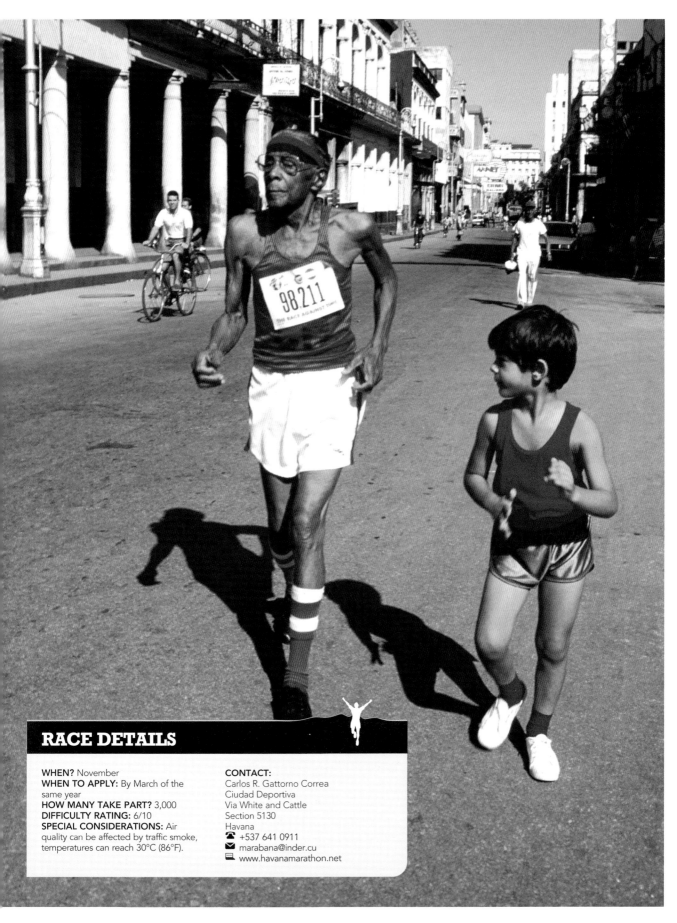

RACE DETAILS

WHEN? November
WHEN TO APPLY: By March of the same year
HOW MANY TAKE PART? 3,000
DIFFICULTY RATING: 6/10
SPECIAL CONSIDERATIONS: Air quality can be affected by traffic smoke, temperatures can reach 30°C (86°F).

CONTACT:
Carlos R. Gattorno Correa
Ciudad Deportiva
Via White and Cattle
Section 5130
Havana
☎ +537 641 0911
✉ marabana@inder.cu
🖳 www.havanamarathon.net

Chicago Marathon | USA

First held in 1977 as Mayor Daley's Marathon, this event became established as 'America's Marathon' in the early 1980s. Britain's Steve Jones set a world record in 1984, grabbing the attention of elite runners looking for a fast course, but by 1987 uncertainties in sponsorship led to funds running low and fewer elite runners took part. Although the race continued to be held annually, it had no sponsor in 1991–2. Then Lasalle Bank took up the title sponsorship and ploughed in enough funding for the race organisers to be able to secure appearances by some of the world's best runners. Chicago has since become a venue to rival London, New York and Boston, as world records were set by Khalid Khannouchi in 1999, Catherine Ndereba in 2001 and Paula Radcliffe in 2002.

More than 4,200 runners turned out for the inaugural race in 1977, making the Chicago Marathon the largest in the world at the time. In recent years it has edged into place as the second largest marathon in the world with over 40,000 runners participating.

WHILE YOU'RE THERE

After expending all those calories, explore the culinary delights of this city, from the pasta delights of **Little Italy** to indulging in a burger at the **Millennium Park Grill**. The Chicago Marathon is an occasion to experience the many great tastes of Chicago. Immediately following the race, runners can celebrate their accomplishment at the **27th Mile Post-Race Party** in Grant Park. All adult runners receive a complimentary 312 Urban Wheat Ale from Chicago's own Goose Island. See: www. gochicago.com

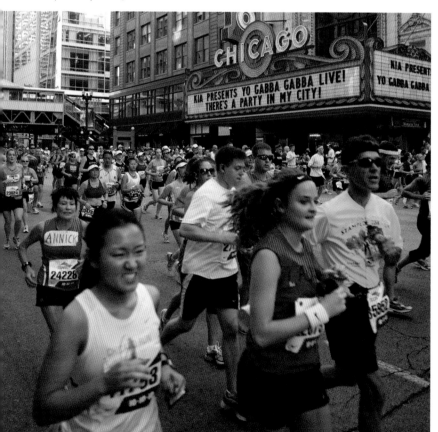

Left: The crowds never thin out on this mass-participation marathon.

Right: Downtown Chicago offers some great distractions to tiring runners.

Over page (top): On marathon day Chicago comes out in force to support the marathon participants.

Over page (bottom): High-fives and street entertainment go hand-in-hand with the best marathons.

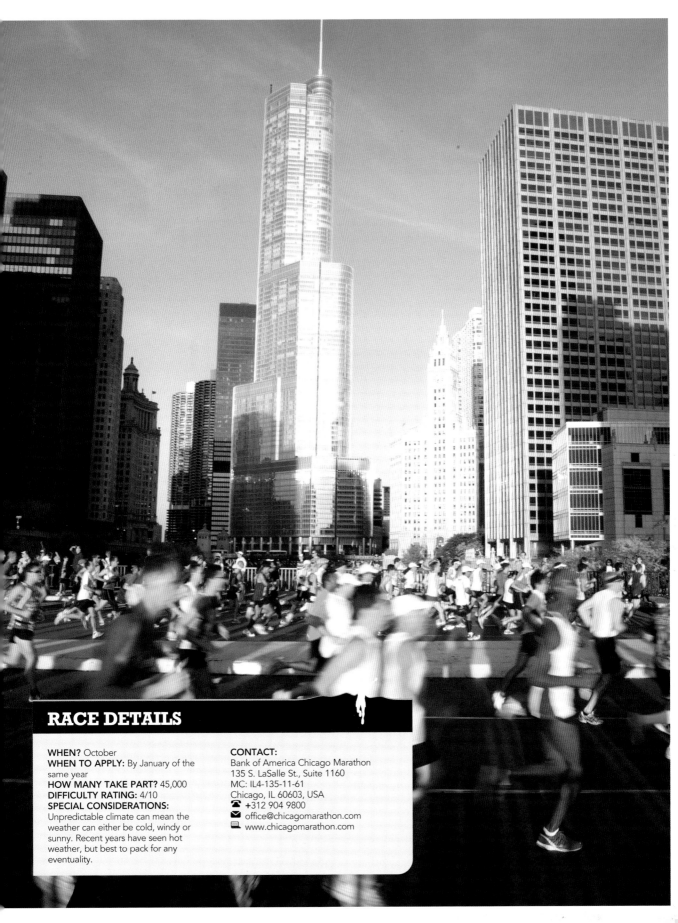

RACE DETAILS

WHEN? October
WHEN TO APPLY: By January of the same year
HOW MANY TAKE PART? 45,000
DIFFICULTY RATING: 4/10
SPECIAL CONSIDERATIONS:
Unpredictable climate can mean the weather can either be cold, windy or sunny. Recent years have seen hot weather, but best to pack for any eventuality.

CONTACT:
Bank of America Chicago Marathon
135 S. LaSalle St., Suite 1160
MC: IL4-135-11-61
Chicago, IL 60603, USA
☎ +312 904 9800
✉ office@chicagomarathon.com
🖥 www.chicagomarathon.com

The course is flat, beginning in the city centre and winding through all the distinctively different ethnic neighbourhoods. Local residents make their presence felt at every stage of the course, vying to become the area offering the most enthusiastic support. Attractions include the male cheerleaders in Boystown, Fleet Feet's Elvis impersonator in Old Town, Old Street Pat's Church in the West Loop, the Mariachi band in Pilsen, and the dancing dragons in Chinatown.

The marathon route passes by several famous landmarks, including the 110-storey Willis Tower (the second-tallest building in North America), the Chicago Theatre on State Street, Lincoln Park Zoo, the Charles J. Hull House and Wrigley Field.

The loop configuration of the course allows spectators to watch runners from more than one spot. With a downtown start and finish, runners and spectators alike can walk from their hotel to the start and back from the finish, avoiding the trouble of taking transport.

The 'windy city' in fact offers quite favourable conditions for running, as proved by the world records achieved here. October temperatures average a high of 16°C (61°F) and a low of 8°C (46°F).

Mazatlan Marathon | Mexico

The start line of the Gran Maratón Pacifico in Mazatlán in Mexico's north west looks more like a gathering of pilgrims than a race. There are young and old, people in wheelchairs and on crutches, blind people and the deaf, all taking part in an event that is a testimony to inclusiveness and the triumph of the human spirit over adversity.

Mazatlán, in the state of Sinaloa, is known as the Pearl of the Pacific, for its beaches and its rich marine fauna. The weather in Mazatlán is hot, with an average daily high in December of 26°C (79°F).

The race was started in 1999 when the Pacific Brewery decided to mark its centenary by organising an athletic event as part of a wider celebration of local culture. The route had one prerequisite, to take in Mazatlán Pier – the longest in the world and one that commands sweeping views of the Pacific Ocean.

The marathon is the main event, but there are races to suit everyone: 5km, 10km, a half marathon, and a 10km event for wheelchair users. In its short history the race has drawn some of Mexico's best-known marathon runners, including Dionicio Cerón and Germán Silva.

51

WHILE YOU'RE THERE

There are beaches by day at an area called **The Golden Zone**, as well as a thriving nightlife. One way to see a different slice of life is to take a boat tour to **Stone Island**, with 20km (12½ miles) of open beach lined with coconut palms. There are plenty of **thatched restaurants** where you can soak up the relaxed atmosphere, or have a well-earned beer while swaying in a hammock. There is also nightlife in town, with live music in bars such as **Joe's Oyster Bar**. See: www.mazatlan.travel

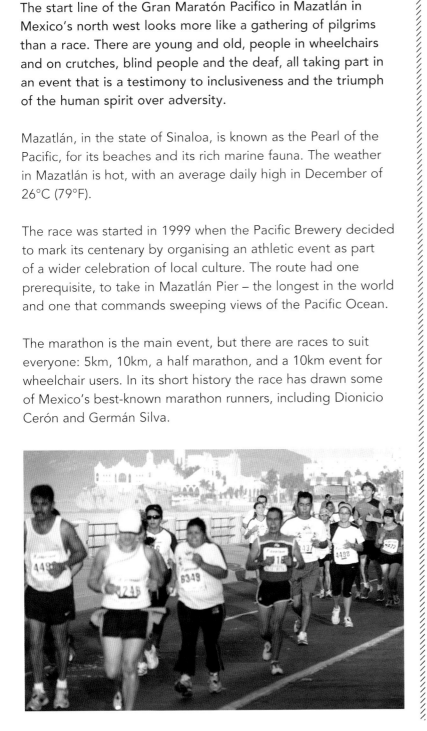

Left: There is a scenic course along the coast in Mazatlán, but beware as it can it be windy and hot.

Hydration is a concern in the high temperatures so water stations are placed every 2km (1½ miles) along the route where the runners can find ice, water and glucose energy drinks. There are three 'run-through' shower stations along the route – and a shower has never felt so reviving as it does here. The medical service is a major operation with 10 specialist sports physicians and 120 paramedics on call for all runners.

The Festival of Light, of which the marathon forms part, is organised by the Pacific Brewery (one of their brews is 'Pacific Light') and the Tres Islas Hoteliers' Association of Mazatlan. The festival offers one of the greatest firework displays in the Americas. There is also a pre-event carbo-loading feast, where around 10,000 guests tuck into plates of pasta, and of course the refreshing beer from the Pacific Brewery that gave rise to the whole marathon adventure.

Above: A wheelchair race runs alongside the main even at the Mazatlan Marathon.

Right: The race through the colonial town is open to all.

RACE DETAILS

WHEN? December
WHEN TO APPLY: May
HOW MANY TAKE PART? 6,500
DIFFICULTY RATING: 6/10
SPECIAL CONSIDERATIONS: Heat can be an issue. Stock up on energy drinks in case of scarcity on race day.

CONTACT:
Gran Maratón Pacifico
Plaza Maratones S.A de C. V.
Río Pánuco No. 157, Col Cuauhtémoc
CP 06500, Mexico D. F.
☎ +525 5280 1716
🖳 www.maraton.org

Big Sur International Marathon | USA

Big Sur is a 145km (90 mile) stretch along the Californian coast from the Carmel River in the north to the San Carpoforo Creek in the south. The Big Sur International Marathon started in 1986 when race founder Bill Burleigh stopped to ponder a simple road sign at the junction of Rio Road and the coastal Highway 101. As a Big Sur resident and runner he knew that running a marathon into the town of Carmel (former mayor: Clint Eastwood) along Big Sur, one of the most gorgeous stretches of coastline in the world, would be a surefire winner. The inaugural marathon drew a crowd of 1,800 and provided a spectacular backdrop of rolling hills, rugged Pacific coastline, and geological and meteorological forces that would daunt anyone without a marathon mentality.

The exposed nature of Big Sur means that every race day is a challenge. The first question is whether the earth will move; after all, this is the line of the San Andreas Fault. The second is whether the land will slip. That happened in 1998 and in 2011, and involved some fancy footwork by Burleigh and his successor, Wally Kastner, to salvage a workable course. What the weather will bring is another question. Gale-force winds, hail and thick fog are not unusual, although mild temperatures, clear blue skies, and even a gentle breeze from the south encouraging runners to the finishline are equally possible.

WHILE YOU'RE THERE

While you're there, there is no doubt that Big Sur is California's natural wonder, packed with national parks, beaches and coastal walks. **Highway 101** helps you see the lot. Of all the beaches **Pfeiffer Beach** is the best-loved but charges a US $5 entry fee to help keep it in pristine shape, although it is frequently ravaged by winds. More natural beauty abounds in **Los Padres National Forest** and **Point Lobos** for **whale watching**. The big metropolis of **San Francisco** awaits and is 3-hour drive away.

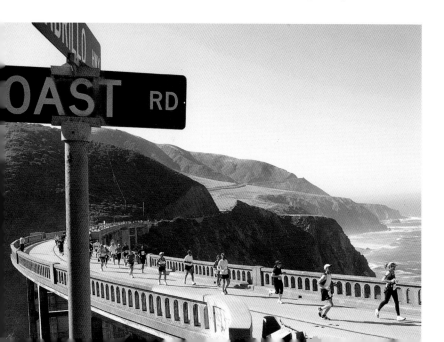

Left: Places in the Big Sur International Marathon sell out fast; this course is not the easiest, but it does have stunning views.

Mother Nature's mischief has never been enough to stop the marathon, but in 1995 floods destroyed the Carmel River Bridge just 200m (650ft) from the finish. A last-minute operation ensured the construction of a temporary structure to allow the show (or 'presentation' in the organisers' parlance) to go on.

The course is unforgettably scenic, passing beneath the majestic redwoods of Big Sur and over gently gurgling streams during the first 8km (5 miles). From there on it gets dramatic. There are mountains on the right-hand side, with green fields and wild flowers in the immediate foreground. On the left lies the Pacific Ocean with its crashing waves and rocky cliffs. If runners look carefully they might be lucky enough to see whales and sea lions, condors, and wild turkeys.

Bill Burleigh obviously appreciated ironic juxtaposition, and introduced an innovative marriage between classical music and wild nature. On the side of the road at the halfway point you will encounter a player at the keyboard of a grand piano.

Below: There are landmarks aplenty on this run, and if you are lucky you may see humpback whales.

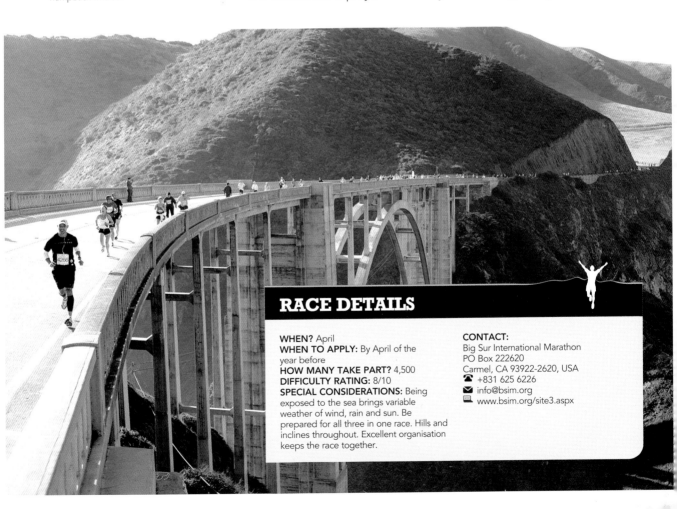

RACE DETAILS

WHEN? April
WHEN TO APPLY: By April of the year before
HOW MANY TAKE PART? 4,500
DIFFICULTY RATING: 8/10
SPECIAL CONSIDERATIONS: Being exposed to the sea brings variable weather of wind, rain and sun. Be prepared for all three in one race. Hills and inclines throughout. Excellent organisation keeps the race together.

CONTACT:
Big Sur International Marathon
PO Box 222620
Carmel, CA 93922-2620, USA
☎ +831 625 6226
✉ info@bsim.org
🖳 www.bsim.org/site3.aspx

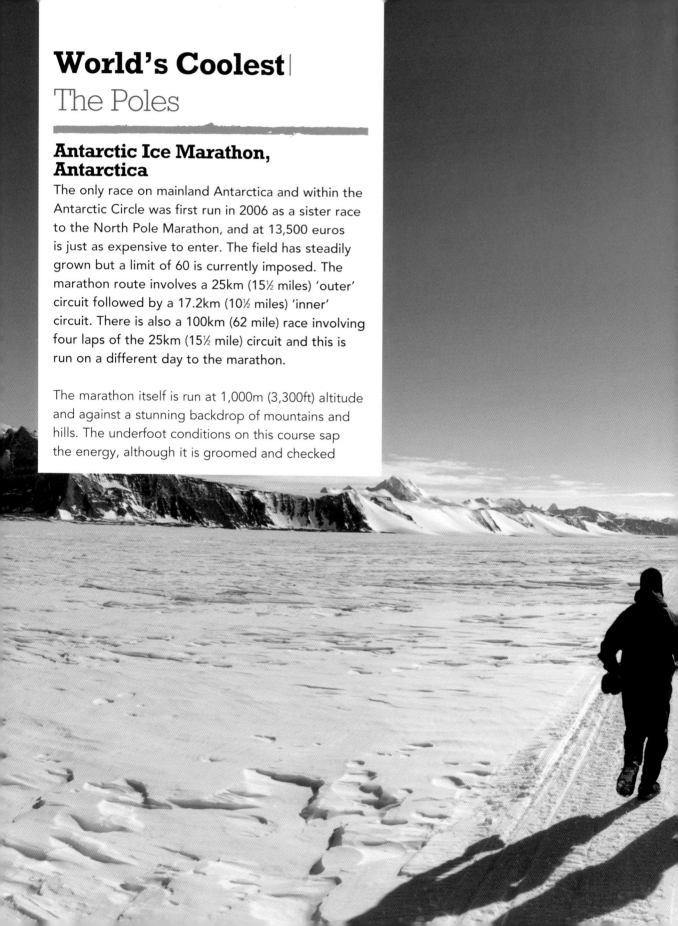

World's Coolest |
The Poles

Antarctic Ice Marathon, Antarctica

The only race on mainland Antarctica and within the Antarctic Circle was first run in 2006 as a sister race to the North Pole Marathon, and at 13,500 euros is just as expensive to enter. The field has steadily grown but a limit of 60 is currently imposed. The marathon route involves a 25km (15½ miles) 'outer' circuit followed by a 17.2km (10½ miles) 'inner' circuit. There is also a 100km (62 mile) race involving four laps of the 25km (15½ mile) circuit and this is run on a different day to the marathon.

The marathon itself is run at 1,000m (3,300ft) altitude and against a stunning backdrop of mountains and hills. The underfoot conditions on this course sap the energy, although it is groomed and checked

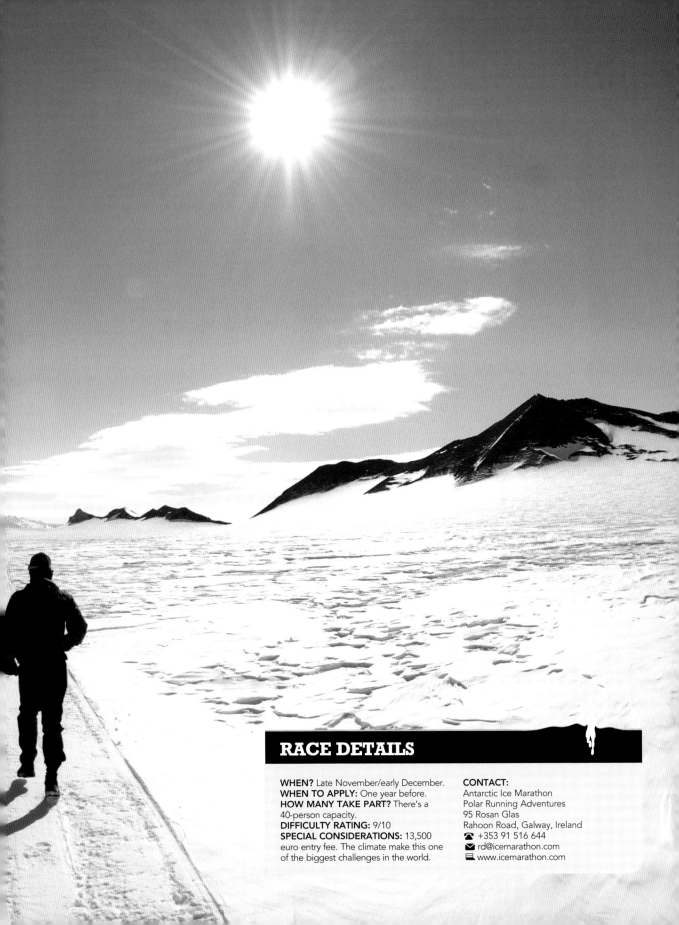

RACE DETAILS

WHEN? Late November/early December.
WHEN TO APPLY: One year before.
HOW MANY TAKE PART? There's a 40-person capacity.
DIFFICULTY RATING: 9/10
SPECIAL CONSIDERATIONS: 13,500 euro entry fee. The climate make this one of the biggest challenges in the world.

CONTACT:
Antarctic Ice Marathon
Polar Running Adventures
95 Rosan Glas
Rahoon Road, Galway, Ireland
☎ +353 91 516 644
✉ rd@icemarathon.com
🖥 www.icemarathon.com

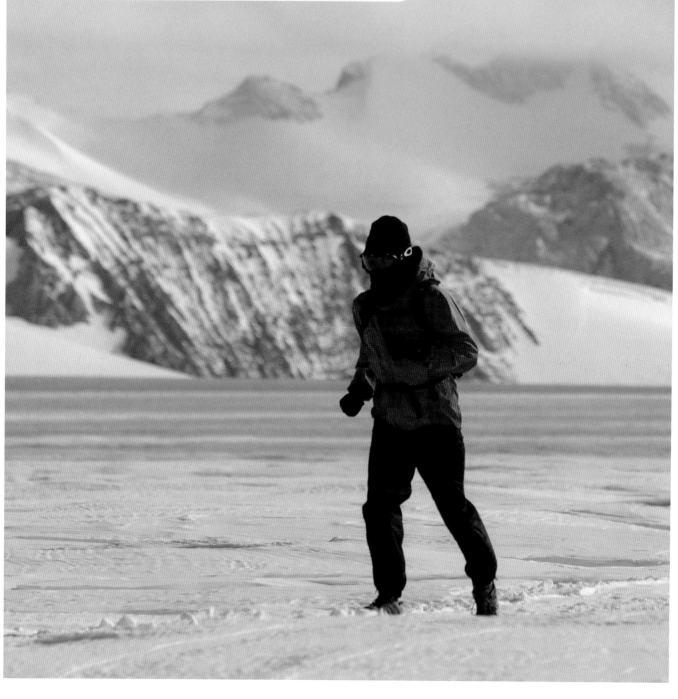

RACE DETAILS

WHEN? First week of April
WHEN TO APPLY: Two years in advance.
HOW MANY TAKE PART? 54
DIFFICULTY RATING: 9/10
SPECIAL CONSIDERATIONS: By no means your average marathon. -30°C (–22°F) temperatures and a 13,500 euro entry fee, you run on ice not land.

CONTACT:
North Pole Marathon
Polar Running Adventures
95 Rosan Glas
Rahoon Road
Galway, Ireland
☎ +353 91 516 644
✉ rd@npmarathon.com
🖥 www.npmarathon.com

for crevasses before the race, which usually takes place in November. Competitors sometimes combine the trip with climbing Mount Vinson (the highest mountain in Antarctica) or flying onward to stand at the precise geographic South Pole. The temperature is typically between -10 and -20°C (14 and -4°F) at its coldest. There is no wildlife here, in fact there is no life at all – penguins can be found at the coast but do not venture into the forbidding interior of the Antarctic. The sense of remoteness is magnified during the race, as there is no sound except the wind, and your own breathing.

North Pole Marathon, Arctic

Make way for the James Bond school of marathons. Think about being dispatched by helicopter, running over ice, and traversing the domain of polar bears. The race may be 'the world's coolest marathon', but it is also the world's costliest. The price of 13,500 euros does not even include the trip to the jumping-off point in Svalbard, at 80° North. Even so, running this marathon is the least expensive way to visit the North Pole.

The challenge is to run on the frozen Arctic ice cap. The race date is governed each year by the establishment of a Russian camp, which is created by a specialist Russian logistics company

WHILE YOU'RE THERE

For many, just being in these extreme reaches of the world is an experience in itself. Unlike most marathon destinations, the terrain is desolate and unpredictable. Runners come here, not just to delight in having ventured so far, but to run long distance where few people have been before. To add to the novelty, there's 24 hours of daylight at both events. Celebrations run wild afterwards. For the North Pole Marathon there's a vodka party at the Pole after the race and many celebratory drinks on the athletes' return to Spitsbergen, Norway. For the Antarctic Ice Marathon, there's usually a big party in the dining tents after the race... and the nightlife in Punta Arenas is enjoyed both before and after the trip.

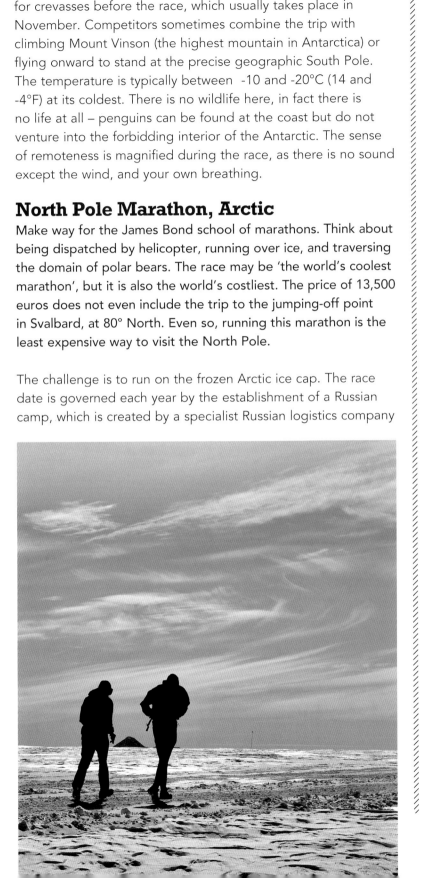

Left: The North Pole Marathon is an extreme, ultra-endurance event for those with astonishing fitness levels and a deep pocket.

Far left: This course is only appropriate for experienced runners.

airdropping a tractor and parachuting personnel onto the ice to construct a landing runway.

The underfoot conditions can be difficult in places as runners must negotiate small hillocks of ice known as 'sastrugi' to complete the marathon. The course is well flagged and carefully arranged to avoid any breaks in the ice or 'leads' that expose the ocean. There is 24 hours of daylight during the event, which is normally held at the end of the first week of April – the most likely temperature is -25°C (13°F) with clear blue skies. Expect no crowd support, except for the few Russian personnel stationed at the camp. For safety reasons, the route is a multi-circuit course typically in the region of 5km (3 miles). Polar bears are a remote threat and guns are kept at camp to deal with any such possibility. The scenery is spectacular with endless miles of ice and a sun that never sets. It is a surreal experience for those that take part.

Below: Camaraderie is strong among this small band of marathon runners.